KEYS TO UNDERSTANDING
SOCIAL SECURITY
BENEFITS

Thomas L. Dickens, Ph.D., CPA, CMA
Professor of Accounting
Clemson University

and

D. Larry Crumbley, Ph.D., CPA
Shelton Taxation Professor of Accounting
Texas A & M University

All inquiries should be addressed to:
Barron's Educational Series, Inc.
250 Wireless Boulevard
Hauppauge, New York 11788

Library of Congress Catalog Card No. 91-21947

International Standard Book No. 0-8120-4466-5

Library of Congress Cataloging-in-Publication Data

Dickens, Thomas L.
    Keys to understanding social security benefits / by Thomas L. Dickens,
D. Larry Crumbley.
        p.   cm.—(Barron's retirement keys)
    Includes index.
    ISBN 0-8120-4466-5
        1. Social security—United States.   2. Old age pensions—United States.
    3. Retirement—United States.   I. Crumbley, D. Larry.   II. Title
    III. Series.
    HD7125.D53   1991
    368.4—dc20   91-21947
                                                                        CIP

PRINTED IN THE UNITED STATES OF AMERICA
2345   5500   987654321

CONTENTS

INTRODUCTION

The intent of the Social Security System is to provide a *basic level* of financial support and health care for the elderly, the disabled, survivors, and those with low incomes. To that end, the Social Security System consists of the following five programs:
1. retirement benefits
2. disability benefits
3. survivors benefits
4. medicare coverage
5. Supplemental Security Income (SSI)

The Social Security System faced financial troubles in the 1970s and early 1980s that were caused by inflation and other economic problems. The economy subsequently has improved, and there have been increases in Social Security taxes. The Social Security System is now in better shape.

Social Security benefits are intended only to replace a portion of a worker's preretirement or predisability earnings. The amount of one's Social Security benefits depends on a worker's level of earnings over his working lifetime. The replacement rate of a retiree's preretirement earnings ranges from about 60 percent for a worker who has always earned the minimum wage to about 26 percent for a worker who has always earned the maximum that counts for Social Security purposes. The benefit formula is thus weighted in favor of low earners to compensate for their lesser ability to accumulate private savings during their working years. Disability benefits should replace about the same proportion of a worker's predisability earnings as would retirement benefits.

The two financial sides of the Social Security System are the contributions taken in and the expenditures to implement the System's programs. Currently, the contributions exceed the expenditures. The excess (called "reserves") is invested in Treasury bonds.

Through the System's five programs, individuals may be eligible to receive Social Security payments at any age. Currently, about 39 million people (16 percent of Americans) receive Social Security benefits. During 1990, these Americans collected more than $240 billion in Social Security benefits.

Information about these five programs, however, is getting more difficult to obtain from the government. With large budget deficits, less money to improve efficiency is being provided to the appropriate governmental agencies. Yet, at the same time more and more people are eligible to draw these benefits.

The purpose of this book is to provide the necessary information to help you understand Social Security and Medicare. However, the laws, regulations, procedures, and available information are constantly changing. Thus, only the Social Security Administration can give you the absolutely correct answer to all questions. Also, if you have special problems with applying for or obtaining your benefits, you might want to consider engaging an attorney who is knowledgeable in the Social Security law. Special problems may relate to receiving disability benefits (especially if the person must go to a hearing), proving paternity to collect a child's benefits on the father's account, and proving retirement from a closely held corporation or family business.

1

FINANCIAL ASPECTS

The five programs that make up the Social Security System—retirement benefits, disability benefits, survivors' benefits, Medicare coverage, and Supplemental Security Income—provide a financial base for the items each is designed to cover. You cannot, however, rely on Social Security to completely fulfill the needs of any one area.

The 1935 Social Security Act reflected the concerns that legislators had with the plight of older, poor workers. This concern was driven by the inability of programs already in place to successfully relieve old-age dependency. The Depression had generated some phenomena that created old-age dependency, such as some companies' ceasing payments to retired workers, the inability of local relief organizations to provide sufficient help, and the overwhelming burden placed on organizations in the private sector to accommodate the needs of older workers. Although older workers' retirement needs were the focus of the original Act, there were also provisions in it that covered others—the blind and the unemployed workers, for example.

The original purpose of adopting a system that required the current working generation to pay to support older, retired workers has remained intact. The original legislation, however, has been modified a number of times by subsequent legislation, giving us the Social Security system we have today. It has been consistently recognized that Social Security benefits are not a cure-all for retirement, disability, and medical problems (as well as nonworking survivors' and dependents' needs), but they make a significant contribution.

The fact that Social Security will provide only a base of support requires every worker to consider and plan for retirement and disability income long before the need arises. Remember that the financial aspect of the retirement years will largely be a result of the planning that has gone before, and insufficient planning or no planning at all usually leads to a less-than-adequate retirement, from a financial standpoint.

The planning entails two steps: (1) arriving at an estimate of the worker's projected income during those periods and (2) determining the extent of the worker's financial needs at that time.

Planning for retirement and possible disability should begin early. Start by requesting from the Social Security Administration (SSA) a projected estimate of your benefits. (An updated estimate should be requested periodically.) Factor into this estimate an approximation of income from an employer's pension and any other income sources, to arrive at the total possible income already in place.

The next step is determining how much income will be needed to supplement Social Security benefits, in order to maintain the desired life-style. In addition to normal cost-of-living expenses, anticipated medical expenditures and supplemental health insurance costs should be included in the estimate, as well as desired discretionary spending. At this point, planning for the investments to produce the balance of the required income can begin.

The Social Security Administration has a convenient procedure for answering questions. One of the SSA's thirty-seven teleservice centers throughout the country can be reached by calling (800) 2345-SSA. For questions that cannot be answered over the telephone, ask for the number of the nearest local Social Security office so you can arrange an appointment.

One important question about Social Security is eligibility. This issue is covered in the next Key.

2

ONCE YOU ARE ELIGIBLE

If you become eligible to receive disability, survivors, Supplemental Security Income, or other benefits, you should apply as soon as you are eligible. To reach the Social Security Administration, call 800-2345-SSA, or check your telephone directory for the nearest of the 1,300 offices.

Here is a list of forms that you may need for the various types of benefits:

- Form SSA-1 F6: Retirement insurance benefits
- Form SSA-2 F6: Wife's or Husband's insurance benefits
- Form SSA-4 BK: Child's insurance benefits
- Form SSA-5 F6: Mother's or Father's insurance benefits
- Form SSA-8 F4: Lump-sum death payment
- Form SSA-10 BK: Widow's or Widower's insurance benefits

The Social Security Administration suggests that you sign up for retirement benefits about three months before you want your benefits to start. It also indicates that almost all of your Social Security business can be handled by telephone, saving time and travel expenses. You may call between 7 A.M. and 7 P.M. The best time to call is right after the middle of the month, and then after the middle of the week, in the afternoon. Representatives are most often cooperative and willing to help you.

When applying for any Social Security benefit, you will have to provide certain documentation, which may include the following:

- Your Social Security card
- Your birth certificate
- Your children's birth certificates (if they are applying)
- Your marriage certificate (if you are signing up for Social Security benefits on your spouse's Social Security record)

- Your most recent W-2 Form, or your federal income tax return (if you are self-employed)

If you do not have the original documents, you must have your copy certified by the issuing office.

Social Security payments can either be mailed to you or deposited directly into your bank account. Direct deposit probably speeds up the availability of the funds to you and is convenient for people who are frequently away from home. If you plan to have your Social Security check deposited directly into your bank account, remember that you will need your checkbook or other papers that show your bank account number when you apply for your Social Security benefits.

There are several procedures to follow in dealing with the Social Security Administration. You should:

1. establish a file for your transactions with them.
2. note the name of the service worker with whom you deal.
3. record dates and names of people working on your claim.
4. make and retain copies of all documents sent to the Social Security office.
5. put your claim number on all documents sent to the Social Security office.

3

DOCUMENTATION IS IMPORTANT

Social Security is intended to provide a *basic level* of support. Whether it is retirement, disability, or survivors benefits received from the Social Security System, those funds are not intended to be the recipient's sole source of income. Social Security payments are intended to *supplement* pensions, insurance, savings, and other investments that the recipient already has.

Your Social Security number is used to keep track of your Social Security earnings and of benefits paid to you from the Social Security System. A 1990 tax law required that all dependents who were at least one year old at the end of the year have a Social Security number, and that the number be shown on the parents' federal income tax return. If you need to get a Social Security number for someone, if you have lost your Social Security card and need another one, or if you need to change the name on your card because of marriage, divorce, or some other reason, contact your local Social Security office and complete Form SS-5, "Application for a Social Security Card."

Bring the necessary documentation to avoid making more than one visit to the Social Security office. For example, if you are getting a Social Security card for the first time, you should have a birth certificate and one other form of identification. You will need the original birth certificate or a certified copy because the Social Security Administration will not accept uncertified copies. A second form of identification for a newborn child may be a doctor or hospital bill.

If you have lost your Social Security card and need a new

one, you will also need identification. If you were born outside of the United States, you must also provide proof of U.S. citizenship or lawful alien status.

If you need to change the name on your Social Security card, documentation is needed. For example, a marriage certificate is necessary if the name change is due to marriage, or divorce papers if the name change is due to a divorce. The Social Security Administration specifies that it will need two documents: one with your old name and one with your new name.

Acceptable forms of identification include the following:
- driver's license
- U.S. government or state employee identification card
- passport
- school ID card, record, or report
- marriage or divorce record
- health insurance card
- medical clinic or doctor records
- military records
- court order for name change
- adoption records
- church membership or confirmation record
- insurance policy

The Social Security Administration will not accept a birth certificate or hospital record as proof of your identity.

4

YOUR PAYMENTS

There are five programs under the Social Security System (see Key 1). While you work, your Social Security taxes are collected to pay for all of these programs except the Supplemental Security Income program. The SSI program is funded with general tax revenues and not Social Security taxes. You pay separately for the retirement, disability, and survivors program on the one hand, and Medicare on the other hand.

In 1991, employees paid 6.2 percent of their gross salary up to $53,400 for the retirement, disability, and survivors programs. Employees paid 1.45 percent up to $125,000 for Medicare. In other words, an employee pays 7.65 percent of his first $53,400 of gross salary into Social Security, and 1.45 percent of his next $71,600 of gross salary into the system. For example, if your gross wages were $92,000, you paid $4,644.80 in Social Security taxes in 1991. This amount is computed as follows: $4,085.10 (7.65 percent of the first $53,400) plus $559.70 (1.45 percent of $38,600 [$92,000 – $53,400]).

For self-employed persons, the Social Security (self-employment) tax rate is 15.3 percent of the first $53,400 of net earnings, and 2.9 percent of excess net earnings up to $125,000. The rates for self-employed persons are double those specified for employees in the previous paragraph. Generally, a self-employed person has self-employment income only if net earnings are at least $400 for the taxable year. If a self-employed person had net earnings of $92,000 in 1991, self-employment taxes would be $9,289.60, which is exactly twice the amount for the employee with wages of $92,000.

Self-employed persons, however, receive two special deductions with respect to their self-employment tax. Both deductions reduce the tax burden on self-employed individuals. One is an *income tax deduction* in computing adjusted gross income on the individual federal income tax return (Form 1040). This deduction equals one-half of the self-employment tax. The deduction was taken on line 25 of Form 1040 for the 1990 and 1991 tax years. Since this deduction is an adjustment for calculating adjusted gross income, several other itemized deductions may be increased: medical expenses, casualty losses, employee business expenses, and miscellaneous deductions.

The deduction for one-half of the self-employment tax may affect the amount of several tax credits, because the credits are affected by the amount of adjusted gross income, which is lowered by the deduction. The credits that may be affected are the child-care credit, earned-income credit, and the credit for the elderly and permanently and totally disabled.

A second deduction (which is *not* an *income tax deduction*) is taken to compute net earnings from self-employment. This deduction equals 7.65 percent of net earnings from self-employment, and was taken on line 4 of Schedule SE for the 1990 tax year.

Assume that Mr. Smith's sole income is from a grocery store that he owns and operates as a sole proprietor. In 1990, he had a net profit from the grocery store of $50,000. Mr. Smith would be allowed a 7.65 percent deduction in computing his self-employment tax. Therefore, only $46,175 [$50,000 − (7.65 percent × $50,000)] of his profit would be subject to the self-employment tax. Thus, his self-employment tax would be $7,064.78 ($46,175 × 15.3 percent). Also, Mr. Smith would be able to deduct $3,532.39 ($7,064.78 × 50 percent) in computing his taxable income.

5

DETERMINING ELIGIBILITY

You must work and pay Social Security taxes to receive Social Security benefits. However, dependents and/or survivors, though they may not have paid Social Security taxes, may receive Social Security benefits through the taxes paid by another person who was covered by Social Security.

You should distinguish between determining eligibility for Social Security benefits and determining the amount of the Social Security benefit. Eligibility for Social Security benefits depends on earning Social Security credits. A person earns credits by working in a job covered by Social Security and paying Social Security taxes. Two things are important:

1. whether your work is covered by Social Security and
2. the amount of earnings on which Social Security taxes are paid.

This Key looks closely at the work that is covered by Social Security. Generally, most jobs are covered by Social Security, but special rules apply to the following:

1. domestic employees
2. farm employees
3. nonprofit organization employees
4. church or church-controlled organization employees
5. federal employees
6. family-member employees
7. self-employed persons
8. military employees
9. the clergy (see Key 43)

In applying the special rules, you must be careful to distinguish between an employee and an independent contractor.

An independent contractor, even though closely resembling an employee, has no employer paying Social Security taxes. Such a person is considered self-employed and therefore subject to the self-employment tax.

The wages of a *domestic employee* in a private household may be covered by Social Security. If one employer pays at least $50 to an employee in a three-month calendar quarter, those wages are covered, but only if the employer and the employee report the earnings. If the earnings are not reported, they will not be covered.

There are at least two situations in which the wages of a *farm employee* are covered by Social Security. First, if a person is hired to do farm work by an employer and the employer spends less than $2,500 a year on agricultural labor but the person is paid at least $150 in cash, those wages are covered by Social Security. Farm work also includes domestic work on a farm. Second, if an employer spends $2,500 or more during the year on agricultural labor, wages paid to hired farm workers are covered by Social Security.

Generally, employees of *nonprofit organizations* are covered by Social Security if they are paid at least $100 in a year. In some instances, employees of certain churches and church-controlled organizations are treated as self-employed persons. Churches or qualified church-controlled organizations can elect in certain situations to be exempt from Social Security taxes. An employee of such a church is still covered by Social Security if at least $100 in a year is earned working for the church or the organization. However, the employee is considered to be self-employed and therefore has to pay self-employment taxes. Earnings are considered self-employment income, even if less than $400.

Formerly, *federal employees' wages* were not covered by Social Security, but the wages of most federal employees hired after December 31, 1983, are now covered by Social Security.

Various rules exist for *family-member employees*. In the following instances, wages are covered by Social Security:

1. a child who is at least 18 and works in a parent's trade or business.
2. a spouse who works in a spouse's trade or business.
3. a parent who works in a son or daughter's trade or business.

Further special rules apply to household work done by a parent for a son or daughter. If you are in this situation, contact the Social Security Administration by calling 800-2345-SSA or visiting your local office.

The self-employment income of *self-employed persons* is covered by Social Security if net profit is at least $400 for the year, and sometimes if it is under $400. Contact the Social Security Administration to determine whether your self-employment income counts for Social Security.

Many special rules apply to *military employees*. Basic pay received by one who is in the military service *after 1956*, for example, is covered by Social Security in the same manner as the income of civilian employees. Also, additional earnings credits may be applied if the credits would result in a higher benefit amount for military employees or if necessary for the family to qualify for benefits.

The manner in which the additional earnings credits are granted depends on when active-duty basic pay was received. If active-duty basic pay was paid in a calendar quarter during 1957–1977, the additional earnings credit is $300 for each calendar quarter in which pay was received. If active-duty basic pay was earned after 1977, the additional earnings credit is $100 for each $300 of active-duty basic pay. No more than $1,200 in earnings credits may be granted for a year. No additional earnings credits are granted for inactive duty training (for example, weekend drills). Other special rules for military employees can be found in Social Security Administration Publication Number 05-10072.

11

6

YOUR SOCIAL SECURITY CREDITS

The amount of the Social Security benefit depends on a number of factors, including date of birth, the type of benefit (retirement, survivors, or disability), and earnings. Normally, earnings are averaged over most of the working lifetime. (Social Security earnings are covered in Key 8 and the amount of the Social Security benefit is covered in Key 13.) Before the amount of the benefit is determined, the worker must qualify for the benefit. Qualification for a particular benefit depends on the number of Social Security credits earned and the worker's age.

Social Security credits are earned as the employee works and pays Social Security taxes. In 1991, one credit was earned for each $540 in Social Security earnings. The amount needed to earn one credit, however, is adjusted for inflation periodically, and it normally goes up every year. In the past, the covered Social Security earnings necessary to earn one credit has increased as follows:

YEAR	SOCIAL SECURITY EARNINGS
1985	$410
1986	$440
1987	$460
1988	$470
1989	$500
1990	$520
1991	$540

Four credits is the maximum number that can be earned in any one year, *regardless of the amount of Social Security earnings*; once the required number of credits to qualify for a benefit are earned, excess credits do *not* affect qualification or the amount of the benefit. (However, the amount of annual earnings ultimately may affect the amount of the Social Security benefit.) The number of credits and a person's age normally determine qualification. The credits necessary to receive retirement benefits have been as follows:

YEAR AGE 62 IS REACHED	CREDITS NEEDED
1986	35
1987	36
1988	37
1989	38
1990	39
1991 or later	40

Suppose Ms. Smith turned 62 in 1991 and had 49 Social Security credits, qualifying her for Social Security retirement benefits. (The amount of the benefit is determined under a separate independent calculation.) On the other hand, if Ms. Smith turned 62 in 1991 and had only 33 Social Security credits, she would not qualify for Social Security retirement benefits under the normal rules.

The credits needed are different if the employee works for a nonprofit organization that was mandatorily covered by Social Security beginning in 1984. (This special rule does not apply if you declined Social Security coverage when it was offered by your employer.) If you were at least 55 years of age and employed by the organization on January 1, 1984, the credits necessary to receive Social Security retirement benefits are:

AGE ON JANUARY 1, 1984	CREDITS NEEDED*
55 or 56	20
57	16
58	12
59	8
60 or older	6

*Must be earned after January 1, 1984.

7

SURVIVORS AND DISABILITY BENEFITS

Survivors benefits are paid in full if a worker has sufficient credits to qualify for retirement benefits. However, in some situations, survivors benefits may be paid even though the worker does not have sufficient credits. The credits that are necessary depend on the employee's date of birth.

If a worker was born *before 1930,* one credit must have been earned for each year after 1950 up to the year in which the worker dies. If the worker was born *in 1930 or later,* one credit must have been earned for each year after age 21 up to the year in which the worker dies.

Where there are dependent children, the date on which a worker was born does not matter as long as six credits were earned during the three years before death. If the worker satisfies this credit/time-period requirement, monthly payments will be made to the surviving dependent children. Family members who qualify for Social Security disability benefits on the worker's record, however, do not need work credits.

In addition, a worker's widow or widower may also be eligible for benefits if that person cares for children who are either under age 16 or disabled. For this situation to apply, the children must be entitled to benefits based on the deceased worker's earnings.

Qualification for *disability benefits* depends on how old the worker is when the disability occurs. There are three age-group categories that determine qualification and relate to disability benefits. They are:

1. *Disability occurs before age 24*: If the worker becomes disabled before turning 24 years of age, six credits must have been earned during the three-year period just prior

to disability. Assume that Mr. Smith became disabled in 1990. He had Social Security earnings of $1,000 in 1988, $1,100 in 1989, and $1,300 in 1990. Since Mr. Smith would have earned two credits for each of the three years up to the year in which he was disabled, *he would qualify* for Social Security disability benefits.

2. *Disability occurs from age 24 through age 30*: If the worker becomes disabled between ages 24 and 30, Social Security credits must have been earned for one-half of the time between age 21 and the disability. Assume that Mr. Smith is 28 when he becomes disabled in 1990. Mr. Smith could have earned a maximum of 28 credits between age 21 and age 28 (four credits each year for the seven years). If he has at least 14 Social Security credits when he becomes disabled, he *qualifies* for Social Security disability benefits.

3. *Disability occurs at age 31 or later*: First, the same number of credits are necessary as are required to qualify for retirement benefits. The following table shows the number of credits needed for people who were *born after 1929* and became disabled at a particular age:

AGE AT WHICH WORKER BECOMES DISABLED	CREDITS NEEDED
31 through 42	20
44	22
46	24
48	26
50	28
52	30
53	31
54	32
55	33
56	34
57	35
58	36
59	37
60	38
62 or older	40

15

The following table shows the number of credits needed if birth was *before 1930* and disability occurred before 62 years of age.

YEAR WORKER BECOMES DISABLED	CREDITS NEEDED
1986	35
1987	36
1988	37
1989	38
1991 or later	40

Second, 20 of the credits must have been earned during the 10 years before disability occurred. Assume that Mr. Smith became disabled during 1991 when he was 42 years of age. If he had at least 40 Social Security credits *and* at least 20 of those credits were earned during the ten years before he became disabled (that is, 1981–1990), he qualifies for Social Security disability benefits.

The rules for qualifying for disability benefits are complex. Also, there is the issue of when a person is disabled (for Social Security purposes). Therefore, people applying for Social Security disability benefits almost always need an attorney, especially if they must go to a hearing. Be sure that your attorney is knowledgeable in Social Security law.

A special rule applies for a worker who becomes disabled before 31 years of age, recovers, and then becomes disabled again at 31 or older. Also, there is a special rule for someone disabled because of blindness. Refer to Social Security Administration Publication Number 05-10072 for the effects of these special rules.

A worker's spouse and unmarried children may also be entitled to receive Social Security benefits based on the worker's Social Security earnings record. These benefits are available to family members if the worker has retired or become disabled, is covered by Social Security, and is entitled to benefits. This rule may apply to children under 18 years of age, children who become disabled before 22 years of age and continue to be disabled, and children who are 18 or 19 years of age and attend elementary or secondary school on a full-time basis.

With regard to *Medicare,* be aware that Medicare medical insurance is separate from Medicare hospital insurance. A monthly premium must be paid in order to receive *Medicare medical insurance.* Generally, anyone who is at least 65 years of age *or* is eligible for Medicare hospital insurance can enroll for Medicare medical insurance. Medicare is covered in greater detail in Keys 21 through 26.

A worker becomes eligible for Medicare hospital insurance at age 65 if any one of these three conditions is met:

1. The worker is entitled to receive monthly Social Security benefits or Railroad Retirement benefits.
2. The worker has worked long enough under the Social Security System or the Railroad Retirement System.
3. The worker has worked long enough as a federal, state, or local government employee to be insured for Medicare purposes.

Also, disability or permanent kidney failure before 65 years of age will qualify a worker for Medicare hospital insurance.

8

SOCIAL SECURITY EARNINGS

Once you have qualified for Social Security benefits by acquiring a sufficient number of Social Security credits, the amount of your Social Security earnings becomes important. This sum is determined by a number of factors including date of birth, the type of benefit for which you are applying, and most important, your Social Security earnings.

A very specific estimate of your Social Security benefit can be obtained from the Social Security Administration. To request that estimate, obtain Form SSA-7004 ("Request for Earnings and Benefit Estimate Statement") from your local Social Security office or call 800-2345-SSA. The address and telephone of the nearest Social Security office is in your telephone directory under "Social Security Administration" or "U.S. Government." The key information needed to complete Form SSA-7004 is:

1. your name as shown on your Social Security card (including other names you have used on Social Security cards).
2. your Social Security number (including all Social Security numbers you have used).
3. your actual Social Security earnings and net self-employment income covered by Social Security for the most recent year.
4. your estimated Social Security earnings and net self-employment income covered by Social Security for the current year.
5. estimated age at which you plan to retire.
6. your estimated average future annual earnings.

Verify your Social Security record about every three years so you can make sure that you are getting credit for all of your earnings. If you are not, the sooner you can identify any inaccuracies, the easier it will be to correct them. To correct an error, you must notify the Social Security Administration within three years, three months, and fifteen days after you discover the error.

An important aspect of Social Security earnings in determining your future Social Security benefits is that the benefits are based on your earnings averaged over most of your working lifetime. This is an important difference from many private pension plans, which may base your retirement benefit on your earnings average over a short part of your working lifetime. For example, a private pension-plan retirement benefit may be based on your earnings averaged over the five years just prior to retirement. Thus (with respect to Social Security), higher lifetime earnings result in higher benefits. If you had some years of no earnings or low earnings, your benefit amount may be lower than if you had worked steadily over your working lifetime.

The first step in computing your benefit is determining the number of years of earnings to use as a base, and this figure depends on the type of benefit you are seeking. With respect to *retirement benefits,* if you were born after 1928 and retire after 1990, the number of years of earnings used as a base is 35 years. If you were born before 1929, fewer than 35 years is used. As for *disability and survivors benefits,* most of the years that are posted to your Social Security earnings record are used.

The second step in computing your Social Security benefit is adjusting the earnings determined at the first step for inflation. These adjusted earnings bear a truer relationship to your earnings at the time you retire, begin receiving disability benefits, or die.

The third step is computing your average adjusted earnings by dividing the earnings total (from the second step) by the number of years (from the first step).

Finally, the average adjusted earnings (computed in the

third step) is multiplied by a percentage, which is specified by law. The percentage is weighted toward low-income workers who have less opportunity to save and invest during their working years. It is about 42 percent for people who have had "average" earnings during their working years. The percentage is lower for workers with higher average earnings, and is higher for workers with lower average earnings.

If you have not accumulated enough Social Security credits to qualify for Social Security, you may be eligible for the Supplemental Security Income (SSI) program. Also, if your benefit from Social Security is very small, you may be eligible for the SSI program. The SSI program is discussed in Key 27.

9

RETIREMENT BENEFITS

If a worker has enough credits to qualify for Social Security retirement benefits, the amount of the benefits depends on when the worker retires. No retirement benefits are paid until a worker has earned the required number of credits; there is no proportionate amount of benefits for a proportionate number of credits earned. Also, any credits in excess of those necessary for full retirement benefits do not increase the amount of the worker's benefit. Only the income that is earned while working increases the benefit amount.

Periodically, the amount of your Social Security benefit is increased, because the Social Security law provides for automatic cost-of-living increases. After you begin receiving benefits, the amount is increased automatically if and when the cost of living increases.

While Social Security benefits are normally paid to a worker who is retiring, they may also be paid to members of the retiring worker's family. Benefits may be paid to a worker's unmarried children who are not yet 18 years of age (or if in high school, not yet 19). Also, benefits may be paid to unmarried children of a worker if the children are older than 18 and were severely disabled (and continue to be disabled) before age 22.

Benefits may be paid to a worker's spouse if the spouse is at least 62 years old and benefits may be paid to the spouse if younger than 62 and caring for their child (who is not yet 16 years old) if the child is receiving Social Security benefits on the worker's Social Security record. The child may be 16 or older if disabled.

The full retirement benefit for your spouse is one-half of your own full retirement benefit. This amount is reduced if

21

your spouse takes benefits before age 65, but it is never lower than 37.5 percent of the worker's full benefit (which applies if the spouse is 62 years of age). Sometimes a circumstance occurs in which a worker is doubly eligible for benefits—under one's own work record and also as a spouse. In this case, the larger of the two benefits will apply. One cannot collect retirement benefits under two separate work records.

You are eligible to receive full retirement benefits if you retire at "full retirement age," which is *now* 65. The amount paid at full retirement age is referred to as "full retirement benefit" (see Key 10). If you retire before age 65, you may be able to receive reduced benefits (see Key 11). Finally, your Social Security benefits may be affected if you take a late retirement. If you do delay your retirement, do not neglect to apply for Medicare at age 65. The reason for doing so at that time is that your medical insurance may cost more if you wait until after age 65 to register for it. See Key 12 for planning opportunities.

If you must retire early because of poor health, you should consider applying for disability benefits. You will have to qualify under the provisions of the disability program (see Key 14), but if you qualify, the amount of your disability benefit is the same as a full, unreduced retirement benefit.

If you mistakenly gave an incorrect birthdate when you originally applied for your Social Security number, this error may be a problem when you apply for your retirement benefits. There is no penalty for the error but you will need to provide at least two items of evidence to establish your true date of birth.

10

FULL RETIREMENT

Workers born before 1938 are entitled to full Social Security retirement benefits at the age of 65. For workers born after 1937, there will be a gradual increase in the age (with age 67 being the highest) at which one is entitled to full Social Security retirement benefits beginning in the year 2000. Below are some examples of when a worker is entitled to *full retirement benefits* under the Social Security System.

YEAR OF BIRTH	AGE AT WHICH ENTITLED TO FULL BENEFITS
1937 or earlier	65 years, 0 months
1938	65 years, 2 months
1939	65 years, 4 months
1940	65 years, 6 months
1941	65 years, 8 months
1942	65 years, 10 months
1943–1954	66 years, 0 months
1955	66 years, 2 months
1956	66 years, 4 months
1957	66 years, 6 months
1958	66 years, 8 months
1959	66 years, 10 months
1960 or later	67 years, 0 months

The following table contains some examples of approximate monthly benefits that a worker would receive at full retirement age, assuming the worker had steady lifetime earnings. These estimates will vary depending on a worker's pattern of earnings in the past as well as the earnings pattern in the future.

AGE IN 1991	1990 EARNINGS		
	$20,000	$40,000	$51,300 or more
	Monthly Benefit Is:		
45	$863	$1,263	$1,422
55	783	1,106	1,195
65	725	982	1,022

The monthly benefit in the table is increased for a worker with a spouse. Moreover, the total benefit for both worker and spouse is increased even more if the spouse qualifies for a higher retirement benefit based on his or her own work record. Finally, there is a provision in the Social Security law for automatic cost-of-living raises. In other words, once a worker begins receiving Social Security benefits, the benefits are increased automatically as the cost of living rises.

A worker does not have to wait until the specified age to retire but Social Security benefits will be reduced for those who retire early. See Key 11.

11

EARLY RETIREMENT

You may begin receiving Social Security benefits as early as age 62, the earliest retirement age, but the benefits to be received are reduced. The reduction in monthly benefits is a percentage for each month prior to what is considered full retirement age (as indicated in Key 10). The earlier you retire, the more the future payments are reduced.

The reduction in benefits is based on the number of months over which Social Security checks will be received before the worker reaches *full retirement age*. Currently, full retirement age is 65. If a worker takes an early retirement at age 62, the monthly Social Security retirement check is reduced by 20 percent. If the worker retires at age 63, the reduction is 13-1/3 percent. And at age 64, it is 6-2/3 percent.

As full retirement age goes beyond 65 years of age, workers will still be able to take an early retirement at age 62. However, since there will be more months in the gap between early retirement and full retirement age, the reduction in monthly Social Security benefits will be greater. The gap mentioned here affects workers born after 1937.

Assume that you have earned enough Social Security credits to qualify for retirement benefits. If you were born before 1938, your age for full retirement benefits is 65. If you retire early, perhaps at age 64, your monthly benefits will be 93-1/3 percent of what full retirement benefits would have been. If you retire even earlier, at age 62, your monthly benefits will be 80 percent of the full retirement benefit.

The following example illustrates the reduction as the gap between full retirement age and early retirement grows. If you take early retirement at age 62 (when the full retirement age is 65), you would receive 36 checks before reaching the full retirement age (three years times 12 monthly checks a year). Your monthly Social Security check will be reduced by 20 percent. However, if you take an early retirement at age 62 in 2027, when the full retirement age will be 67, you would receive 60 checks before reaching your full retirement age (five years times 12 monthly checks a year). Your monthly Social Security check will be reduced by 30 percent.

There are several items to consider regarding early retirement and reduced Social Security benefits. First, what is the total amount of other retirement benefits? Planning during preretirement years is important in this regard in order to maintain your standard of living in retirement.

Second, what Social Security benefits are available to your spouse? Remember that if you receive a reduced Social Security benefit, your spouse's retirement benefit will also be reduced. However, if your spouse could receive a larger retirement benefit based on his or her own work record, a reduced benefit on your own record may be unimportant.

Third, to what extent will your Social Security benefits be reduced if you receive non-Social Security income during your retirement years? If that income is in interest or dividends, for example, your Social Security payments will not be affected, but if it is wage- or salary-related, your benefits will be reduced. From age 62 to 65, benefits are reduced $1 for every $2 earned, but from age 65 to 69, the reduction is $1 for every $3 earned. This phenomenon requires careful preretirement planning.

And remember, if you choose to take a reduced benefit before age 65, the monthly payment remains the same after age 65.

12

PLANNING RETIREMENT AGE

There are planning opportunities available concerning the Social Security benefits a worker will receive upon retirement. The distinct disadvantage of retiring early is that monthly benefits are reduced. However, the potential advantage is that benefits are received for a longer period of time. Generally, a worker who retires early should receive about the same total lifetime Social Security benefits as a worker who retires at full retirement age. Social Security planning must be done within the context of overall planning for retirement.

A potential planning opportunity involves a worker whose poor health forces early retirement. Since an early retirement will result in reduced Social Security benefits, the worker should consider applying for Social Security disability benefits wherein the amount of the disability benefit is the same as a full, unreduced retirement benefit. (Read about disability in Key 14.)

There are two considerations for the worker who is thinking of *late retirement*. First, depending on what is earned each year beyond the normal age for Social Security retirement, average earnings may be increased. (Recall from Key 8 that an increase in average earnings could result in an increase in your Social Security benefit when you retire.)

Second, there is a special credit for late retirement that causes an increase in retirement benefits. The increase, based on a certain percentage, is automatically added to the Social Security retirement benefits, from the time of full retirement age, until the worker begins to take benefits or reaches age 70, whichever comes first.

This special credit varies depending on the year in which

the worker was born. For those who turn 65 in 1991, the percentage is 3.5 percent for each year beyond normal retirement age. The percentage increases in the future, until it ultimately reaches eight percent per year for employees who turn 65 in 2008 or later. The following table shows the increases for workers who delay their retirement.

YEAR OF WORKER'S BIRTH	ANNUAL PERCENTAGE INCREASE
1916 or earlier	1.0%
1917–1924	3.0%
1925–1926	3.5%
1927–1928	4.0%
1929–1930	4.5%
1931–1932	5.0%
1933–1934	5.5%
1935–1936	6.0%
1937–1938	6.5%
1939–1940	7.0%
1941–1942	7.5%
1943 or later	8.0%

As an example, workers born in 1943 or later receive an extra eight percent benefit each year they delay retiring beyond full retirement age.

As indicated in Key 22 on Medicare, if a worker plans to delay retirement beyond age 65, the Social Security Administration should be contacted two to three months before retirement so that Medicare hospital insurance protection will begin at 65. One or more months of available Medicare medical insurance protection could be lost and in some instances medical insurance will cost more if a worker delays applying (refer to Key 23).

Of course, when a worker chooses to retire is a decision unique to each individual situation. One should consider any private pension benefits, the reduction in benefits for early retirement, the Social Security credit and private pension plan mechanisms for delaying retirement, the ability to continue working, the personal financial situation, and health insurance implications.

Whether a worker takes an early retirement, a normal retirement at age 65, or a delayed retirement, once the decision to retire has been made, the Social Security application process must be started. A worker should apply for Social Security retirement benefits at least two or three months before the actual retirement date.

To begin the application process, call or visit the nearest Social Security office. Look under "Social Security Administration" or "U.S. Government" in the telephone book. If you have trouble locating the office, call the Social Security Administration's toll-free number, 800-2345-SSA.

Generally, if you apply for early retirement and reduced benefits, the benefits will start no earlier than the month in which you apply. If you delay applying until after you have reached 65, back payments are usually paid for up to six months, but back payments are not paid for the months before you reached age 65. These implications make it especially important to contact the Social Security Administration several months before you wish your benefit payments to begin.

To facilitate the application process, be sure to have the necessary documentation (outlined in Key 2) when applying for retirement benefits. If your spouse is also applying for benefits, similar documentation is required.

13

ESTIMATING YOUR BENEFITS

The Social Security Administration provides estimates of Social Security benefits, which can be obtained by completing and mailing Form 7004-PC, available at any Social Security office or by calling the Social Security Administration's toll-free number, 800-2345-SSA.

The amount of your monthly Social Security retirement check can be estimated. Although the calculation is complex, it is worth making and comparing against the computerized amount provided by the Social Security Administration. The two amounts may differ slightly. If you do not agree with the computerized amount, you may request a reconsideration, but the request must be timely.

Generally, your Social Security benefit is based on your wage and salary earnings averaged over most of your working lifetime. Therefore, nonearning amounts (interest, dividends, rentals, and Social Security income) are not counted. However, trade or business net income on which you pay self-employment tax (Schedule SE on your federal income tax return) does count.

The following model calculation is based on the assumption that you reach age 62 after 1990. The monthly figure generated using this model is only an approximation, because there will be future changes in the cost of living and wages. Also, this model cannot be used to estimate benefits accurately if you become eligible after 1985 for a pension based on work not covered by Social Security.

First, count 35 years of earnings. (The younger you are, the more years of earnings you will have to estimate.)

Second, take the lower of your actual earnings or the maximum earnings subject to Social Security for each year.

Compute this for each year up to the year in which you plan to retire, estimating your annual earnings for 1992 and later years. As the table below indicates, use the 1992 amount as an estimate of the maximum earnings subject to Social Security beyond 1992. These earnings for earlier years are provided in the following table:

YEAR	MAXIMUM EARNINGS SUBJECT TO SOCIAL SECURITY
1951–1954	$ 3,600
1955–1958	$ 4,200
1959–1965	$ 4,800
1966–1967	$ 6,600
1968–1971	$ 7,800
1972	$ 9,000
1973	$10,800
1974	$13,200
1975	$14,100
1976	$15,300
1977	$16,500
1978	$17,700
1979	$22,900
1980	$25,900
1981	$29,700
1982	$32,400
1983	$35,700
1984	$37,800
1985	$39,600
1986	$42,000
1987	$43,800
1988	$45,000
1989	$48,000
1990	$48,000
1991	$53,400
1992 and later	$53,400

Third, adjust the annual figures calculated in step two by an inflation factor. The factors for each year are:

YEAR	FACTOR	YEAR	FACTOR
1951	6.6	1969	3.1
1952	6.2	1970	2.9
1953	5.8	1971	2.8
1954	5.8	1972	2.6
1955	5.6	1973	2.4
1956	5.2	1974	2.3
1957	5.1	1975	2.1
1958	5.0	1976	2.0
1959	4.8	1977	1.9
1960	4.6	1978	1.7
1961	4.5	1979	1.6
1962	4.3	1980	1.5
1963	4.2	1981	1.4
1964	4.0	1982	1.3
1965	3.9	1983	1.2
1966	3.7	1984–1986	1.1
1967	3.5	1987 and later	1.0
1968	3.3		

Fourth, take the 35 years of highest annual earnings and add the earnings to get your total earnings. Compute your average indexed monthly earnings by dividing the total earnings by 420 (35 years times 12 months per year).

Finally, compute the estimate of your monthly benefit at a retirement age of 65 by using the table on page 33.

With early retirement, the estimated average monthly retirement benefit is reduced permanently. The amount of the reduction depends on the number of months benefits are received before age 65 (see Key 11).

If you retired at age 62, your monthly benefit would be reduced by 20 percent, so you would receive 80 percent of the estimated average monthly retirement benefit. If you retired at age 63, you would receive 86-2/3 percent of the

AVERAGE INDEXED MONTHLY EARNINGS	AVERAGE MONTHLY RETIREMENT BENEFIT
$339 or less	.9 × average monthly earnings
$340 – $2,044	$305.10 + (.32 × [average monthly earnings – $339])
more than $2,044	$850.70 + (.15 × [average monthly earnings – $2,044])

estimated average monthly retirement benefit and if you retired at age 64, you would receive 93-1/3 percent of the estimated average monthly retirement benefit.

Consider also that your spouse is entitled to receive Social Security monthly retirement benefits. Your spouse's benefit (based on your Social Security work record) equals one-half of your age-65 benefit. If your spouse is not yet 65 years old when you begin receiving benefits at 65, your spouse's monthly benefit will be permanently reduced. As with the worker's permanent reduction, the spouse's reduction depends on the number of months benefits are received before age 65. The reduction equals 25 percent at age 62 when the benefits begin, 16-2/3 percent at 63, and 8-1/3 percent at 64.

14

DISABILITY BENEFITS

A number of disability benefits are available through the Social Security System. Some examples include benefits for:

1. workers who have earned sufficient Social Security credits to qualify on their own work records.
2. the disabled widows or widowers who had earned sufficient Social Security credits to qualify on their own work records.
3. workers with low income and few assets who might be eligible for Supplemental Security Income benefits.
4. children over age 18 who might be eligible based on the parents' work records.
5. children at any age who might be eligible based on qualification for Supplemental Security Income benefits on their own. (Because the disability rules for children have recently been rewritten, and new standards for evaluating their disabilities have been developed, special attention should be paid to possible benefits for disabled children. The general intent of the revised rules is that more children with disabilities may qualify for benefits, especially Supplemental Security Income benefits.)

Workers covered by Social Security can receive Social Security disability benefits *at any age*. If workers are receiving disability benefits when they turn 65 years of age, the disability benefits become retirement benefits and the amount remains the same.

Two categories of disability benefits are available to family members in certain situations: family members who qualify for disability benefits on the worker's record *when the worker is living* and those who qualify for benefits on the worker's record *when the worker dies*.

There are four specific situations in which the worker's family members may qualify for disability benefits when the worker is living:

1. If the worker has an unmarried son or daughter who is disabled, the child would qualify to receive benefits. The worker's stepchild, adopted child, and in some cases, grandchild, will qualify if under age 18, or if the child is a full-time high school student under age 19.

2. If the worker has an unmarried son or daughter who is age 18 or older with a disability that began before age 22, the child will qualify. If a child under age 18 received disability benefits under Social Security, contact the Social Security office to ensure that the disability checks continue if the disability remains after the child turns 18.

   Workers with disabled children should be aware of the potential Social Security benefits that are available for their children, whether the children suffer from a form of mental retardation or any of numerous childhood conditions. More than 475,000 children who are under age 18 and disabled are now receiving Social Security benefits. Check with the Social Security office to determine what benefits are available.

3. A worker's spouse who is disabled can qualify to receive Social Security benefits on the worker's Social Security record. However, the spouse must be at least 62 years old before the benefits begin.

4. A worker's spouse who is caring for their child can qualify to receive benefits *at any age* if the child is under age 16 or is disabled, and is also receiving Social Security checks.

There are two specific cases in which a worker's family may qualify for disability benefits if the worker dies:

1. The worker's disabled widow or widower qualifies if that individual is at least 50 years old and the disability began before the worker's death *or* within seven years after the worker's death.

2. The worker's disabled ex-wife or ex-husband can qualify for disability benefits if they were married for at least 10 years.

The Social Security System's disability program is one of the most complex. This complexity is why it is often advisable to retain an attorney in applying for disability benefits. If there are any doubts about qualifying for disability payments, first contact the local Social Security office or call 800-2345-SSA.

15

DEFINITION OF DISABILITY

In order to qualify for payments under Social Security's disability program, an individual must have a *physical or mental impairment* that (1) keeps the person from doing any "substantial" work for at least one year or (2) is expected to result in death. The disability program payments are not intended to cover temporary, short-term, or partial disability.

Social Security has such a strict definition of disability because the system assumes that working families have other resources to provide support for temporarily or partially disabled workers, such as workers' compensation, insurance, savings, and investments.

If qualified, a worker may receive benefits based on either blindness or disability, but special rules apply to blind persons. Blindness is defined as vision that cannot be corrected to 20/200 in the better eye, or a visual field that is 20 degrees or less, even with corrective lenses.

In 1991 a blind person could earn up to $810 a month before the earnings were considered "substantial." In other words, the person would not lose Social Security benefits until total earnings exceeded $810 a month.

A blind person who works regularly and has substantial earnings might qualify for a disability "freeze," and should therefore still file for benefits. Under a freeze, future benefits will not be reduced because of relatively lower earnings during the years when a worker was blind. Key 8 explains that future Social Security benefits are computed based on average earnings over the working life. Under a freeze, the lower earnings years when a worker was blind would not be incorporated into the benefit calculation model, and thus future benefits would not be reduced.

Do not confuse Social Security's definition of disability with that of another insurer's, such as a private pension plan or other government disability programs. The fact that a worker might qualify for disability payments from another insurer does not automatically ensure payments under Social Security's disability program. Additionally, a statement from a doctor indicating that a worker is disabled does not ensure payments under Social Security's disability program.

Workers who become disabled and believe they might qualify for payments under Social Security's disability program should file for benefits by contacting their local Social Security office or calling 800-2345-SSA. Claims can be expedited by providing:

1. the Social Security number and proof of age for each person who is applying for Social Security payments. (Be sure to have this information for your spouse and children, if they are applying for benefits.)

2. the names, addresses, and telephone numbers of your doctors, and hospitals, clinics, etc., where you have been treated, as well as the dates of treatments you have received.

3. a summary of where you have worked in the last 15 years, including the kind of work you did in your job(s).

4. a copy of your W-2 Form or (if you are self-employed) your federal income tax return for the past year.

5. the dates of any prior marriages, if your spouse is applying for benefits.

Workers should not delay filing for Social Security disability benefits merely because they do not have all of the necessary information. Because it takes longer to obtain medical information and to assess a worker's ability to work, the claims process for disability benefits is generally longer than for other types of Social Security benefits, usually taking 60 to 90 days. Your claim may be expedited if you have an attorney advise you regarding filing procedures.

16

DISABILITY PROCESS

To determine if a worker is disabled, the Social Security Administration has a process that involves the following five questions.

1. *Are you working?* The Social Security Administration generally will not consider you as disabled if you are working and earning at least $500 a month.

2. *Is your condition "severe"?* Your impairments must interfere with basic work-related activities or your claim for disability benefits will be denied.

3. *Is your condition found in the list of disabling impairments?* The Social Security Administration maintains a list of impairments for each of the major body systems that are so severe that the impairment automatically means you are disabled. If your condition is not on the list, the Social Security Administration must determine if the impairment is equal in severity to an impairment on its list. If it is equal, your disability claim will be approved. If it is not equal, question 4 is asked.

4. *Can you do the work that you previously did?* Remember, at this point it has been determined that your impairment is not as severe as any on the Social Security Administration's list. Now it must be determined if your impairment interferes with your ability to do the work you have been doing for the last 15 years. If it does not, your disability claim will be denied. If it does, question 5 is asked.

5. *Can you do any other type of work?* In assessing your capacity to do another type of work, the Social Security Administration considers the following factors: age, education, past work experience, and transferable skills.

Additionally, it reviews the job demands of occupations as determined by the Department of Labor. If it is found that you cannot do any other kind of work, your disability claim will be approved. Otherwise, your claim will be denied.

A claim may be denied at any of the various steps in the Social Security Administration's review process. If a claim is denied or if the worker disagrees with any other decision the Social Security Administration makes, the decision can be appealed. There are at least four levels of appeal (see Key 17).

If a worker disagrees with the decision at any appeal level, an appeal can be made to the next level within 60 days from the time the decision is received. The Social Security Administration presumes a worker receives a decision five days after it is dated unless the recipient proves otherwise.

17

LEVELS OF APPEAL

There are four levels of appeal for workers who disagree with the Social Security Administration's decision about their disability or other claims:
1. reconsideration
2. hearing
3. Appeals Council
4. U.S. District Court

If you plan to appeal, act promptly. Appeal requests made more than 60 days after a determination are usually not honored.

Reconsideration entitles a worker to have a decision reviewed by people other than those who made the original decision.

A worker, while entitled to apply for a *hearing* before a judge, should be aware of a special consideration. At this point, the need for an attorney should be investigated. A hearing is requested either by writing a letter or by filing Form HA-501. Include the following information:
- name and Social Security number
- reason for disagreement
- statement of any additional evidence submitted
- name and address of attorney (if one has been retained)

If the Social Security Administration has decided that a worker is no longer medically disabled, it may request at the hearing that Social Security disability benefits continue while the hearing decision is pending.

You are responsible for your attorney costs, but if the hearing is more than 75 miles from your home, the Social Security Administration reimburses you for reasonable travel expenses.

If the *Appeals Council* determines that there is an issue the judge did not address at the lower appeal level, it will review the case, but at this point all levels of appeal within the Social Security Administration are exhausted. If the Appeals Council denies a review because it believes all issues have been addressed by the judge at the hearing level of appeal, or if the Appeals Council renders a decision with which a worker disagrees, the worker must appeal to a federal civil court to continue the appeals process. The avenues for appeal after the U.S. District Court are the Circuit Court of Appeals for the applicable district court and, finally, the U.S. Supreme Court, if it agrees to hear the case.

As with each of the steps that are a part of the appeals process, a worker has 60 days from the receipt of the Appeals Council decision to appeal to the *United States District Court* that has jurisdiction over the worker.

18

WHEN DISABILITY PAYMENTS BEGIN

Social Security payments are usually paid on the third of every month and cover the preceding month. Generally, disability payments begin in the *sixth full month* in which a worker is disabled and continue as long as the disability persists. The six-month period begins with the first full month after the onset of the worker's disability. The waiting period does not apply to payments for disabled children or for disability payments under the Supplemental Security Income program.

If a worker is disabled (under Social Security's definition of disability) on April 17 and a claim is promptly filed and approved, the first disability payment may be expected November 3. From a planning standpoint, delays in disability payments can usually be avoided by filing for benefits as soon as possible after the disability occurs.

After disability payments begin, the Social Security Administration will periodically assess the disabled person's health situation to see if it has improved and if so, to what extent. This process involves gathering information about the disability, reviewing health problems, and considering other circumstances.

The information gathered about health simply involves checking with doctors, hospitals, and clinics involved. In some instances, however, the administration may decide it needs more information and may require the person to take a special examination or medical test (at the expense of the Social Security Administration). A special examination is also frequently required prior to a finding by the Social Security Administration that one is disabled.

Disability payments will be discontinued when your condition improves to the point that you no longer are disabled, or you are able to return to "substantial" work. Substantial work is defined as "substantial gainful activity," "substantial" meaning the work involves productive physical or mental activities and "gainful" meaning the work is done for pay or profit. Normally, a worker earning $500 or more a month is engaged in a "substantial gainful activity." Although disability payments will cease, a determination by the Social Security Administration that the worker is engaged in a "substantial gainful activity" will not affect any benefits that might exist under the Supplemental Security Income program. See Key 27.

Other more obvious findings by the Social Security Administration may cause disability benefits to be curtailed or stopped. Such findings might stem from new examinations or tests indicating that the disabled person is not as disabled as in the past and can now work, or the fact that the disabled worker refuses to follow doctor-prescribed treatment that might permit a return to work. Physician-prescribed treatment must be followed to obtain benefits.

Social Security disability payments or other Social Security benefits may also be reduced if the worker is eligible for other government benefits such as workers' compensation or disability benefits from certain federal, state, civil service, or military disability programs. The total payments to worker and family from Social Security and any of these programs cannot exceed 80 percent of the average current earnings of the worker before becoming disabled.

If the worker's widow or widower is disabled and is receiving Social Security disability payments, or if the disabled worker's spouse is receiving Social Security payments, a *government pension offset* may exist. The offset applies if a worker becomes eligible for a federal, state, or local government pension based on work not covered by Social Security. The amount of the spouse's Social Security benefit may be reduced by two-thirds of the amount of the worker's government pension, but there are some cases in which the offset does not apply. The rules for a government pension offset are covered in Key 44.

In a similar vein, if you are disabled and drawing Social Security disability payments, and at the same time you are receiving a monthly pension based on work that is not covered by Social Security, your Social Security disability payment will be reduced. This circumstance is covered in Key 45.

Special rules permit a disabled person to return to work without immediately losing monthly disability benefits and Medicare and Medicaid coverage. These *disability work incentives* can be used to the disabled worker's advantage.

19

DISABILITY WORK INCENTIVES

There are four disability work incentives that may be used if a worker is receiving Social Security disability benefits:

1. trial work period
2. extended period of eligibility
3. deductions for impairment-related expenses
4. Medicare continuation

With respect to the *trial work period* incentive, a disabled worker may earn an unlimited amount for nine months without having any Social Security disability benefits affected. The nine months of work do not have to be consecutive, but they must be within a five-year period in order to be considered a trial work period. A trial work month is any month in which a worker earns more than $200. After nine trial work months, the work is evaluated to determine if it is substantial. Generally, if the average monthly earnings do not exceed $500, the Social Security disability benefits will continue; but if they do exceed $500, Social Security disability benefits will cease after a three-month grace period.

With the *extended period of eligibility*, the worker that is still disabled for 36 months after a successful trial work period will be eligible to receive a monthly benefit without a new application if any monthly earnings drop below $500.

Under the *deductions for impairment-related expenses* incentive, work expenses that are related to one's disability are discounted when determining if the earnings constitute substantial work.

Regarding the *Medicare continuation* incentive, a worker's Medicare coverage continues for 39 months beyond the trial work period. If Medicare coverage stops then, it may be purchased for a monthly premium.

The amount of monthly disability benefits is based on lifetime earnings covered by Social Security. For 1991, the average monthly payment to a disabled worker was $587 and the average monthly payment to a disabled worker with a family was $1,022.

The following table contains some examples of approximate monthly disability benefits that a covered worker might receive under the Social Security disability program. The table assumes the worker was disabled in 1991 and had steady lifetime earnings. These estimates will vary depending on the worker's pattern of earnings in the past. The monthly benefit in the table is greater for the worker with a spouse and children.

	1990 EARNINGS		
AGE IN 1991	$20,000	$40,000	$51,300 or more
	Monthly Benefit Is:		
25	$732	$1,079	$1,202
45	720	1,040	1,105
64	736	997	1,036

After receiving Social Security disability payments for two years, the worker is automatically enrolled in Medicare. Key 21 explains the components of Medicare. The hospital insurance may be free (depending on eligibility), but the employee must pay a monthly premium for the medical insurance.

20

SURVIVORS BENEFITS

Survivors benefits are payments to family members (including a divorced widow or widower) after one's death. The payments, which may involve lump-sum payments as well as annuity-type monthly payments, are based on the deceased person's Social Security record. The deceased person must have earned sufficient credits while working in order for any benefits to be paid.

If a deceased worker had sufficient Social Security credits, a special lump-sum, one-time payment of $255 will be made but the amount is paid only to certain members of the family.

The following are some examples of family members who may be able to collect Social Security payments on a deceased worker's Social Security record:

1. a widow or widower who is at least 60 years old.
2. a widow or widower who is at least 50 years old and disabled.
3. a widow or widower, regardless of age, if caring for a child who is either under 16 years old or is disabled.
4. unmarried children under age 18.
5. unmarried children age 18 or 19 who are full-time elementary or secondary school students.
6. unmarried children over age 18 who are severely disabled and the disability began before the child was 22.
7. parents, if they are dependent on the deceased worker for most of their support.
8. divorced widows or widowers if they are not eligible for equivalent or higher benefits on their own records. Generally, the widow or widower may not be currently married (unless the remarriage occurred after the widow or

widower reached 60 years of age). (It should be noted here that if remarriage occurred after age 60, the ex-spouse, widow, or widower will be eligible for a widow's benefit on the worker's Social Security record, or a dependent's benefit on the new spouse's record.) Also, the widow or widower must be at least 60 years old (50, if disabled) and must have been married to the deceased worker for at least 10 years. However, it does not matter how old the widow or widower is if that person is caring for a child who is eligible for benefits on the deceased worker's Social Security record.

There are limits on the monthly payment amount to survivors. Although the limit varies, it is usually about 150 percent to 180 percent of the deceased worker's benefit rate. If the benefits payable to one's surviving family members exceed the limit, the benefits to family members are reduced proportionately.

The amount of a survivor's benefits depends on the earnings of the person who died. As a general rule, the more that the deceased person paid into Social Security, the greater the amount of benefits that survivors will receive.

The table on page 50 contains some examples of the approximate monthly benefits that might be paid to a covered worker's survivors. The table assumes the worker died in 1991 and had steady lifetime earnings. These estimates will vary depending on the worker's pattern of earnings in the past.

Survivors' benefits can be quite substantial. For example, suppose a worker died in 1990 at age 35, had earned about $35,000 in 1989, had maintained an average earnings pattern during his working life, and is survived by a wife and two children (ages 8 and 10). Without considering cost-of-living increases, the deceased worker's family could receive more than $177,000 in Social Security benefits before the younger child is 18 years of age.

AGE IN 1991	1990 EARNINGS		
	$20,000	$40,000	$51,300 or more
	Monthly Benefit Is:		
35, with			
spouse, 1 child	$1,090	$1,610	$1,790
spouse, 2 children	1,338	1,879	2,088
spouse, age 60	519	768	853
45, with			
spouse, 1 child	$1,082	$1,566	$1,670
spouse, 2 children	1,330	1,828	1,948
spouse, age 60	515	713	796
55, with			
spouse, 1 child	$1,086	$1,496	$1,562
spouse, 2 children	1,334	1,745	1,822
spouse, age 60	517	713	744

21

MEDICARE ELIGIBILITY

Medicare is a federal basic health insurance program that covers people age 65 or older, people of any age with permanent kidney failure, and certain disabled people—many regardless of their age. It is operated by the Health Care Financing Administration, although the Social Security Administration takes applications for Medicare, assists beneficiaries in claiming Medicare payments, and provides information about the program. Medicare is not intended to cover all hospital and medical bills. As a matter of fact, today it pays less than half of the average older person's health-care costs.

Medicaid is a health insurance program designed for people with low income and limited assets. It is usually run by state welfare or human-service agencies. Medicaid covers more than 28 million people. It is very costly, with a price tag greater than $90 billion in 1991. It varies widely from state to state. A person may qualify for both Medicare and Medicaid, or for only one of the programs.

There are two parts to Medicare. Hospital insurance is often referred to as Part A; it helps pay for inpatient hospital care and some follow-up care. The hospital insurance is financed through part of the Social Security tax. Medical insurance is often referred to as Part B; it helps pay for doctor's services and many other medical services and items. The medical insurance is voluntary and is financed by monthly premiums paid by those who have enrolled in it and by general federal revenues. The coverage and benefits aspects of Medicare are covered in Key 24.

There are many ways in which a worker may qualify for Medicare benefits. A worker is eligible at age 65 if the worker is entitled to monthly Social Security or Railroad Retirement benefits. However, a person who is at least 65 also qualifies for Medicare if he or she has worked long enough to be insured under Social Security or the Railroad Retirement System. Also, a person at least 65 years old may be entitled to monthly Social Security benefits based on a spouse's work record, but the spouse must be at least 62 years old (the spouse does not have to apply for benefits). Finally, a person who is at least 65 years old and has worked long enough in federal, state, or local government employment to be insured for Medicare purposes, also qualifies for Medicare.

In certain situations a person not yet 65 years old may qualify for Medicare. This category includes persons who have been entitled to Social Security disability benefits for 24 months, and those who have worked long enough in government employment and meet the requirements of the Social Security disability program.

People are eligible for Medicare regardless of age if they need maintenance dialysis or a kidney transplant for permanent kidney failure. However, they must be insured or receiving benefits under Social Security or Railroad Retirement, or must have worked long enough in government employment. Additionally, spouses or children of workers may qualify for Medicare if they need maintenance dialysis or kidney transplants. Medicare coverage is available only to the family member who has the kidney problem.

In other special situations, spouses, divorced spouses, widows or widowers, or dependent parents may qualify for Medicare hospital insurance when they reach age 65. Similarly, certain disabled widows and widowers under 65, disabled surviving divorced spouses under 65, and disabled children who are 18 or older may qualify for Medicare. A person who falls into one of these special categories should contact the Social Security Administration at its toll-free number, 800-2345-SSA.

22

MEDICARE PART A APPLICATION CONSIDERATIONS

The process of applying for Medicare involves two aspects: hospital insurance protection (Part A) and medical insurance protection (Part B).

Some people must apply for the hospital insurance (Part A) before it will start, and for some people it will begin automatically.

There are at least six instances in which an application for the hospital insurance coverage is necessary:

1. You have reached age 65 and *you plan to continue working*. The Social Security Administration recommends that you apply for Medicare about three months before you reach your 65th birthday. To begin the application process, contact any Social Security office or call the toll-free number, 800-2345-SSA.

2. You are a government retiree who is eligible for Medicare on the basis of government employment. To apply, contact the Social Security Administration about three months before you become 65. Follow the procedure outlined in 1 above.

3. You are a widow or widower between 50 and 65 years of age, you are disabled and are receiving other Social Security benefits, and you have not applied for disability benefits. Contact the Social Security Administration and apply immediately, if you qualify for the coverage. Do not delay if you are in this situation, because there is a waiting period for eligibility for the hospital insurance.

4. You are a government employee and you become dis-

abled before you turn 65. In this case, you may qualify for Medicare hospital insurance on the basis of your government employment. Contact the Social Security Administration at once if you fall into this category, because there is a 29-month waiting period for Medicare hospital insurance.

5. You, your spouse, or your dependent child needs kidney dialysis or a kidney transplant. If you are not able to reach the Social Security office to apply, a Social Security representative will come to you and take the application. Simply contact any Social Security office by telephone, or call 800-2345-SSA. Your Medicare hospital insurance protection usually begins the third month after the month in which you actually begin maintenance dialysis treatments, but coverage may begin earlier in some cases.

6. Even if you are not eligible for hospital insurance (Part A) under any of the above five circumstances, you can buy Medicare hospital insurance when you turn 65. To obtain the coverage, you must enroll and pay the monthly premium for medical insurance protection (Part B). If you are an alien, you are required to become a permanent resident and you must reside in the United States for five years before you can purchase Medicare protection. The basic premium for Medicare hospital insurance in 1990 was $175 a month. Remember that Part A hospital insurance incurs a cost only if you do not qualify for free coverage. If you are in this category and want to apply, contact any Social Security office.

23

MEDICARE PART B APPLICATION CONSIDERATIONS

Some people qualify automatically for Medicare medical insurance (Part B) while others must apply for it. Unlike Medicare hospital insurance, if you qualify for Medicare medical insurance and want it, you must pay for it. The basic monthly premium cost was $28.60 in 1990. There really is not a good alternative to Part B coverage and individual medical insurance coverage at age 65 is difficult to buy. Even if it were available, the cost would be prohibitive. Part B is a good buy, value- and eligibility-wise.

Generally, anyone who is at least 65 years old qualifies for Medicare medical insurance and anyone who qualifies for Medicare hospital insurance can enroll for the medical insurance. In other words, a person does not need any Social Security or government work credits in order to qualify for Medicare medical insurance. As with the hospital insurance, aliens who are at least 65 years old must be permanent residents of the United States and must reside in the United States for at least five years before they are eligible to enroll in the medical insurance program.

You are automatically enrolled for Medicare medical insurance protection if you are receiving Social Security benefits or retirement benefits under the Railroad Retirement System, unless you indicate that you do not want it. Your enrollment begins when you become entitled to Medicare hospital insurance (Part A) coverage.

There are a number of instances in which a person may be entitled to Medicare medical insurance protection, but not automatically enrolled. In the following eight situations, a person must apply to receive the Medicare medical insurance protection by contacting a Social Security office (you may call 800-2345-SSA), or the Railroad Retirement office (if appropriate).

1. The worker plans to continue working after age 65.
2. The worker refused Medicare Part B medical insurance protection at the time of eligibility for Medicare Part A hospital insurance protection.
3. The person is 65 years of age and not eligible for Medicare hospital insurance protection.
4. The person has permanent kidney failure.
5. The person is a disabled widow or widower between 50 and 65 years old and is not receiving disability benefits (perhaps because of other Social Security benefits).
6. The person previously had Medicare medical insurance protection, but terminated it for some reason.
7. The person is eligible for Medicare because of government employment.
8. The person lives in Puerto Rico or outside the United States.

There is an initial *enrollment period* of seven months for Medicare's Part B medical insurance protection. The period begins three months before the month of initial eligibility for the medical insurance protection, and ends three months after that month.

For example, assume that Molly Smith turns 65 during June 1992. Molly is single, has never been disabled, and plans to continue to work after age 65. Molly will have to apply for Medicare medical insurance; her initial enrollment period is from March 1992 through September 1992. If Molly wants to enroll in Medicare's medical insurance program when she turns 65, she will have to apply and enroll during the seven-month period from March 1992 through September 1992.

If a person enrolls for the medical insurance protection

during the first three months of the enrollment period, any coverage begins with the month in which he or she becomes eligible for the protection. If enrollment occurs during the last four months of the enrollment period, the coverage begins one to three months after enrollment. In Molly Smith's case, if she enrolls between March and May of 1992, her medical insurance protection will begin in June 1992. If she enrolls between June and September of 1992, her protection will begin one to three months after she has enrolled.

People who do not sign up for the medical insurance protection during their initial enrollment period can enroll during a general enrollment period from January 1 through March 31 of each year. The protection does not begin until the following July and the monthly premium will be 10 percent higher than the basic premium for each 12-month period for which the person could have been enrolled but was not.

Returning to Molly Smith's case, if she had not enrolled during her March-to-September initial enrollment period, she could enroll during the general enrollment period of January 1 through March 31, 1993, or January 1 through March 31, 1994. Her medical insurance protection would not begin until July 1993, or July 1994, respectively.

For the medical insurance enrollment period, special rules apply to workers and their spouses who are 65 or older and have employer group health coverage, and to disabled people who are under 65 and have employer group health coverage. For these special rules, consult the Social Security Administration's Publication Number 05-10043, *Medicare*, or call its toll-free number, 800-2345-SSA.

24

MEDICARE COVERAGE AND BENEFITS DESCRIPTION

As discussed in Key 21, Medicare consists of two parts: (1) Hospital insurance, often referred to as Part A, and (2) Medical insurance, often referred to as Part B.

The four major areas of hospital insurance coverage are:
1. inpatient hospital care.
2. inpatient care in a skilled nursing facility.
3. home health care.
4. hospice care.

With inpatient hospital care, Medicare hospital insurance pays for part of your hospital costs for a limited period of time. That part varies, depending on the time you are in the hospital, but in any event, Medicare helps to pay for only up to 90 days in any participating hospital in each benefit period.

In 1990, Medicare hospital insurance paid for all *covered services* for the first 60 days of your hospital stay in a benefit period. (A benefit period begins on the day you enter a hospital and ends when you are out of the hospital or skilled nursing facilities for sixty consecutive days. A new benefit period begins the next time you enter a hospital.) However, there was a deductible of $592 that year and of $628 in 1991.

The covered services include semiprivate room, all meals, regular nursing services, operating and recovery room costs, hospital costs for anesthesia services, intensive care and coronary care, drugs, lab tests, X rays, medical supplies and appliances, rehabilitation services, and preparatory services related to kidney transplant surgery.

Beyond the first 60 days, there is a different Medicare

rate for inpatient hospital care. For the 61st through the 90th day of a person's hospital stay, Medicare hospital insurance paid for all covered services beyond $148 a day in 1990 and $157 in 1991.

To summarize, for the first 90 days of a person's hospital stay in a benefit period in 1991, Medicare generally paid for all covered services, but there was a flat $628 total deductible for the first 60 days and a daily $157 deductible for each day from the 61st through the 90th day.

Suppose a person covered by Medicare's hospital insurance is in the hospital more than 60 days in a benefit period. The Medicare hospital insurance provides that you can use some or all of your 60 nonrenewable "reserve days" to help defray your inpatient hospital care costs beyond the first 90 days. For each "reserve day" used, Medicare generally pays for all covered services. There was a daily $296 deductible in 1990.

Medicare's Part A hospital insurance protection will pay for a portion of the cost of inpatient skilled nursing or rehabilitation services for up to 100 days after a hospital stay, provided certain conditions are satisfied. In 1990, Medicare generally paid for all covered services for the first 20 days in a participating skilled nursing facility in each benefit period. There is no deductible for the first 20 days. Medicare also paid all covered services beyond a $74 daily deductible for the next 80 days in that year. Covered services for inpatient care in a skilled nursing facility include semiprivate room, all meals, regular nursing services, rehabilitation services, drugs, medical supplies, and appliances.

The Medicare hospital insurance protection program also pays for certain home health care costs. Provided certain other conditions are satisfied, Medicare will pay the full approved cost of home health visits from a participating home health agency if a person is confined to home; there is no limit to the number of covered visits the person can have. Services that are covered under the home health care provision include part-time skilled nursing care, physical therapy, and speech therapy. Also covered are the part-time services of home health aides, occupational therapy, medical social services, and medical supplies and equipment.

Medicare hospital insurance covers the costs connected with a Medicare-certified hospice, but probably not all of the costs if they are connected with outpatient drugs and inpatient respite care. Medicare does cover all of the costs if they are connected with doctors' services, nursing services, medical appliances and supplies (but only part of the cost of drugs), home health aide and homemaker services (but only part of the cost of inpatient respite care), therapies, and medical social services.

Under the medical insurance protection program, Part B, Medicare medical insurance will help the insured to pay for doctor services and a number of other medical services and supplies that might not be covered by the Part A Medicare hospital insurance. People who must use Medicare because of permanent kidney failure will find that many of the services that are needed are covered by the medical insurance protection program.

The medical insurance protection program has both a deductible and a coinsurance provision. During 1990, a person was responsible for the first $75 of the medical insurance-covered costs (the deductible). Beyond the $75 deductible, the medical insurance generally picks up 80 percent of the approved charges for covered services for the year (the coinsurance provision).

25

AREAS OF MEDICAL INSURANCE COVERAGE AND NONCOVERAGE ITEMS

The four major areas of medical insurance coverage are:
1. doctors' services.
2. outpatient hospital services.
3. home health visits.
4. other medical and health services and supplies.

Items covered under doctors' services are surgical services, diagnostic tests and X rays that are part of the treatment, medical supplies furnished in doctors' offices, services of office nurses, and drugs that are administered as part of the treatment (and cannot be self-administered). Medicare's medical insurance payments are based on what the Medicare carrier approves as the "reasonable charge." The approved amount, however, is often less than the doctor's (or other) actual charge.

Medical insurance covers outpatient hospital services that a person receives for diagnosis and treatment. Examples are care received in an emergency room or the outpatient clinic of a hospital.

The number of home-covered health visits is unlimited, but certain conditions must be met and the patient must not be enrolled in Medicare Part A (hospital insurance).

Sometimes the cost of other medical services and supplies is covered. For example, the cost of ambulance transportation, home dialysis equipment, supplies, periodic support services, independent laboratory tests, outpatient physical therapy and speech pathology services, and X rays and radiation treatments might be covered in this area.

While Medicare's hospital and medical insurance programs cover many of the costs connected with illness, some are not covered. Remember that Medicare is designed to afford basic protection against the high cost of illness—not to pay all of one's health care expenses.

A doctor or provider who accepts assignments usually files Medicare claims, others may not. After a claim is filed, you will receive notification of the decision the carrier has made. If you disagree with the decision, you have the right of appeal, but there are dollar minimums for Medicare appeals cases. Part A hospital insurance appeals usually begin by requesting a hearing before an administrative law judge of the Social Security Administration. Part B medical insurance appeals usually require a hearing by the insurance carrier before going to the administrative law judge.

The services and supplies that Medicare will not cover include:

1. custodial care (help with bathing, eating, and taking medicine).
2. dentures and routine dental care.
3. certain appliances (such as eyeglasses and hearing aids), as well as examinations to prescribe or fit them.
4. nursing home care, except for care in a skilled nursing facility.
5. personal comfort items (a telephone or television in the hospital room).
6. prescription drugs.
7. most routine physical checkups and related tests.
8. hospital or medical services that are received outside of the United States (Puerto Rico, Guam, American Samoa, the Virgin Islands, and the Northern Mariana Islands are considered part of the United States). Also, the cost of care in certain qualified Canadian or Mexican hospitals may be covered by Medicare, at least in part.

The eight noncoverage areas offer some planning opportunities for people who want to expand their health insurance coverage. When buying private health insurance to supplement Medicare health insurance coverage, people need to be sure that the private insurance does not simply duplicate their Medicare insurance. The Social Security Administration has two publications that can be helpful in deciding to supplement Medicare with private health insurance. The publications are *A Guide to Health Insurance for People with Medicare*, and a fact sheet entitled "Should You Buy a Supplement to Medicare?" Among other information, these publications identify the types of supplemental insurance that are available. See Key 26.

26

PURCHASING INSURANCE TO SUPPLEMENT MEDICARE

As Keys 24 and 25 indicate, there are a number of hospital expenses and medical expenses that Medicare covers and some that it does not cover. Noncovered expenses are specified in Key 25.

The areas of noncoverage are caused by "gaps" in Medicare coverage. Gaps can be caused by:

1. deductibles under the Medicare insurance policy.
2. coinsurance amounts specified in the insurance policy.
3. medical charges that exceed Medicare's approved amounts.
4. various medical services and supplies for which Medicare does not pay.

A variety of private insurance policies are available to help pay for medical expenses and services and supplies that Medicare either does not cover or does not cover in full. The basic types of policies include:

1. Medigap insurance (Medicare supplement).
2. hospital indemnity insurance.
3. nursing home or long-term care insurance.
4. specified disease insurance.
5. coordinated care plans (health maintenance organizations [HMO's], competitive medical plans [CMP's]).

Medigap policies are common. The National Association of Insurance Commissioners has established standards that require a Medigap policy to include certain minimum coverages such as:

1. the Part A coinsurance amount, namely $157 per day in 1991 for the 61st through the 90th day of hospitalization in each Medicare benefit period.

64

2. ninety percent of Medicare Part A eligible expenses for a lifetime maximum of 365 days after all Medicare hospital benefits are exhausted.
3. the Part B coinsurance amount, which generally is 20 percent of eligible expenses after the policyholder pays the $100 annual deductible.

Most of the states have adopted minimum benefits standards, but there may be differences in basic Medigap policies from state to state. Therefore, it is extremely important to determine the standards that are in effect in your state and if the standards apply to your Medigap policy.

There are a number of considerations to take into account when shopping for health insurance to supplement Medicare coverage. Some of them are:

1. *Shop carefully before you buy.* Watch for differences in the coverage and cost of policies. Also, be aware that companies differ in services offered. Obtain at least two estimates before purchasing a policy to supplement Medicare. Make sure that you are comparing apples to apples.
2. *Do not buy more policies than you need.* Avoid owning several policies with overlapping or duplicate coverage —a single comprehensive policy is better.
3. *Check for preexisting-condition exclusions.* Although most states require that Medigap policies cover preexisting conditions after the policy has been in effect for six months, many policies do not cover health problems that exist at the time of purchase. Investigate closely what preexisting conditions the policy covers and does not cover.
4. *Determine maximum benefits.* Most policies have some type of limit on benefits. The policy may restrict the dollar amount that will be paid for treatment of a condition, or it may limit the number of days of care for which payment will be made.
5. *Check renewal privileges (or lack of them).* The least permanent coverage is provided by policies that permit the company to refuse to renew your policy on an individual

basis. Good protection is provided by policies that can be renewed automatically. Look for a policy that cannot be canceled because of claims or disputes. Many policies cannot be canceled by the company unless all policies of that type are canceled in the state.

6. *Look for an outline of coverage.* You are required to be given a clearly worded summary of the policy. Be sure to obtain the summary and read it carefully.

7. *Take advantage of the "free-look" provision.* Insurance companies are required to give you at least 30 days to review a Medigap policy. Send the policy back to the agent or company within 30 days of receiving it if you do not want the policy. If you have problems getting a refund, contact your state insurance department.

States are responsible for the regulation of insurance within their boundaries, and various state laws govern insurance carriers and their agents. Federal criminal and civil penalties can be imposed upon any company or agent who knowingly sells someone a policy that substantially duplicates existing coverage, unless the policy also pays duplicate benefits. Also, it is illegal for an individual or company to misuse the names, letters, symbols, or emblems of the U.S. Department of Health and Human Services, the Social Security Administration, and the Health Care Financing Administration.

Anyone who believes they have been victimized by unlawful sales practices should contact the state insurance department. Call the federal toll-free number, 800-638-6833, to register violations of federal law.

27

SUPPLEMENTAL
SECURITY INCOME

This program is often referred to as "SSI." SSI, although run by the Social Security Administration, is not financed by Social Security taxes or trust funds but by general revenue funds of the U.S. Department of the Treasury.

Under the SSI program, SSI checks may be paid to people who are age 65 or older, disabled, or blind, and who have low income and few assets (see Keys 29 and 30 for details on the low-income and assets tests). SSI payments may be made to adults and disabled and blind children.

The Social Security Administration states that blindness includes both those who are totally blind and those who have very poor eyesight. A person who is not considered blind for purposes of receiving SSI payments may qualify to receive checks under Social Security's disability program. Disability occurs if a physical or mental problem prevents a person from working, *and* the problem is expected to last at least a year or to result in death. The disability program is covered in Keys 14–19.

SSI payments may be made to people who have low income and few assets. Additionally, qualifying persons must:
1. live in the U. S. or the Northern Mariana Islands.
2. be a U. S. citizen or live in the United States legally.
3. apply for Social Security or other benefits, if eligible. One might be able to draw Social Security checks in addition to an SSI check.
4. be at least 65 years of age, blind, or disabled. A disabled person must accept vocational rehabilitation service if offered.

28

SSI AND DISABILITY PROGRAM DIFFERENCES

A worker needs to distinguish between disability benefits under Social Security's disability insurance program and the Supplemental Security Income program. The medical requirements for disability payments are the same under both programs, and a disability is determined by the same process under both programs. Also, the two programs are similar with respect to some of the work-incentive rules, including the deductions for impairment-related expenses, discussed below and in Key 19. Basically, this work-incentive deduction discounts expenses related to a worker's disability when computing whether the earnings constitute substantial work.

There are a number of ways in which Social Security's disability insurance program and the Supplemental Security Income program are different. Some of the differences are:

1. Supplemental Security Income disability payments are based on financial need and assume that a person does not have the resources to handle short-term health problems. Therefore, there is no disability waiting period under the Supplemental Security Income disability program. There is a six-month waiting period under Social Security's disability program.

2. Under Supplemental Security Income, a worker may qualify for an immediate disability payment if the condition is obviously disabling and the worker meets the Supplemental Security Income resource and income limits. Refer to Keys 29 and 30 for these limits.

3. As long as the Supplemental Security Income limits are not exceeded, cash benefits and Medicaid will continue.

Under the Social Security disability program, once a worker reaches the level of substantial work, the disability benefits cease.

4. Under the Supplemental Security Income program, money may be set aside for up to 48 months for a work goal.

Eligibility for Social Security disability is based on prior work under Social Security, whereas disability payments under the Supplemental Security Income program are made on the basis of financial need. Refer to Keys 7 and 14 for the specifics of Social Security's disability insurance program. Refer to Key 31 for the specifics of disability benefits under the Supplemental Security Income program.

29

SSI INCOME TEST

To understand the low-income test under the SSI program, the definition of income must also be understood. Income includes:

1. earnings.
2. Social Security.
3. other government checks, pensions, etc.
4. value of noncash items received (the value of free food, clothing, and shelter).

However, the Social Security Administration does not count all income when determining whether a person qualifies to receive SSI under the income test. Items that *are not counted* include:

1. the first $65 a month one earns from working and one-half of the amount over $65 a month.
2. food stamps.
3. food, clothing, or shelter that the person receives from private nonprofit organizations.
4. most home energy assistance.

A disabled person who meets the income and assets tests may receive SSI benefits. If a disabled person is able to work, any wages the person uses to pay for items or services that are needed in order to work because of the disability are *not* counted in implementing the income test. For example, the amount of a worker's wages used to pay for the cost of a wheelchair needed by the worker would not be counted as income. Similarly if wages are used by a blind person to pay for transportation to and from work, that portion of wages would not be counted as income in applying the income test.

If the SSI recipient is married, the Social Security

Administration also takes into account the income of the recipient's spouse. Moreover, if the SSI recipient is under age 18, the income and assets of the recipient's parents may be considered.

In addition to the definition of income, whether or not a person works and the state in which the person lives are important in determining SSI. The amount of income that the recipient can have and still receive SSI benefits depends partly on the state of residence.

A single unemployed person may qualify for SSI benefits if monthly income is less than $427 ($630 for a couple). Usually, income amounts below these figures will qualify the person under the income test, regardless of the state of residence. These amounts are the minimum federal rates. It is possible that the state in which one lives has a higher SSI income rate and, therefore, a higher income limit. As a matter of fact, many states allow much more income than these minimum federal rates. To verify the income rate and income limit for a state, check with the local Social Security office.

If employed, a person is entitled to have more monthly income and still qualify for SSI benefits. If all of one's income is from working, a single worker may qualify for SSI benefits if monthly income is less than $899 ($1,305 for a couple). Again, these amounts are the minimum federal rates, and a given state may have a higher rate and limit.

30

SSI WORKING AND ASSET TESTS

Regarding the low-asset test, a worker must understand the definition of assets. Generally, assets are the things that someone owns. However, all assets are not counted to determine whether an individual qualifies for SSI benefits. For example, a home, usually a car, and many personal belongings are not counted in computing the asset limitation. Common items considered include cash and bank accounts. If an SSI recipient is married, the Social Security Administration also takes into account the assets of the recipient's spouse.

A person may qualify for SSI benefits if the counted assets are $2,000 or less for one person, and $3,000 or less for a couple. Unlike income limits, these limits are not different depending on the state in which a person lives.

The assets that the Social Security Administration considers in applying the asset test include the *value* of the following:

1. real estate
2. personal belongings
3. bank accounts
4. cash
5. stocks
6. bonds

However, the value of everything the taxpayer owns is not counted. The following items are specially treated for purposes of the asset test:

1. The home in which the person lives and the land on which the home is located do not count.
2. Depending on their value, a part or all of one's personal

and household goods and the cash surrender value of life insurance policies may not count.

3. A car usually does not count.
4. Burial plots purchased for oneself and immediate family members do not count.
5. In some cases, up to $1,500 apiece in burial funds for the worker and spouse ($3,000 in total) does not count.
6. The cost of some items for disabled or blind persons who receive SSI benefits may not count if the items are used to enable the person to work or earn extra income.

SSI payments may be made to disabled or blind persons who meet the income and assets tests. There are also special rules that affect a disabled or blind person who receives SSI payments and works. Generally, if a person starts working, SSI checks should decrease or stop. However, sometimes the disabled or blind person who works may set aside earnings to go toward a work goal, or to go to school. Money set aside for these purposes *does not* count in applying the limitations prescribed by the income and asset tests. In other words, the person may be able to set aside the money and not have the SSI benefit reduced or stopped. Anyone in this situation should contact the Social Security Administration at 800-2345-SSA.

31

SSI MONTHLY BENEFITS

The basic monthly SSI benefit from the federal government for 1991 was $407 for one person and $610 for a couple. Also, some states will supplement the basic federal amount. Consequently, some people may receive different SSI amounts, depending on the state in which they live. Some recipients may get a lot more if they live in a state that pays money beyond the basic SSI check.

The basic federal rate is reduced if an SSI recipient lives rent-free in someone else's home or in an institution where room and board are paid for by the state. Also, the SSI recipient may have SSI benefits reduced if there is income from other sources.

SSI benefits may be paid to those with certain disabilities, both workers and their children. The general Social Security rules for determining disability also apply in determining disability for the SSI program. Similarly, the SSI program has special plans to help a disabled person who desires to return to work to do so without the risk of suddenly losing SSI benefits or Medicaid coverage.

The standards for evaluating disability in children were recently revised to enable more children to qualify for SSI benefits. If you have a disabled child who was previously denied SSI benefits, you should consider reapplying for SSI benefits. The disabled child may now qualify for SSI benefits because of the relaxed rules for defining disability.

Persons qualifying for SSI benefits should be aware of other benefits that may be available to them. For example, most recipients of SSI may be able to receive food stamps, Medicaid assistance, or various social services.

More information about Medicaid can be obtained by

contacting a local welfare or medical assistance office. Contact the nearest social services department or public welfare office about social services that may be received. Medicaid assistance can help pay doctor and hospital bills. Medicaid is a different program than Medicare (See Key 21).

The same considerations that are involved when a person applies for Social Security benefits apply when a person applies for SSI benefits. If you believe you qualify for SSI benefits, apply immediately because there are no retroactive benefits.

The Social Security Administration recommends having the following items when applying:

1. your Social Security card (if you do not have a card, then you should have a record of your Social Security number: for example, employer payroll stubs, a copy of a filed federal income tax return, etc.).
2. birth certificate or other proof of age.
3. information about the home where you live (your mortgage if you own or are buying your home, or a lease and your landlord's name if you are renting).
4. payroll slips, bank books, insurance policies, car registration, burial fund records, and other information about your income and your assets.
5. for persons signing up for disability benefits, the names and addresses of doctors, hospitals, and clinics that have seen them, and the names and addresses of social workers or institution superintendents.

Additionally, if you want your Social Security checks to be deposited directly into your bank account, take your checkbook or other items that include your name and account number.

You should apply, however, even if you do not have all of the documents needed to qualify.

32

COMMUNICATION FROM THE SOCIAL SECURITY ADMINISTRATION

As the cost of living increases in the United States, Social Security benefits are adjusted accordingly. Each January, the Social Security Administration will notify recipients of any new benefit amount brought about through a cost-of-living adjustment (COLA).

Outside earnings, representing the amount of earnings you can have and still receive all of your Social Security benefits, can change over several years. As an example, these amounts for 1991 are summarized in the following table:

AGE	OUTSIDE EARNINGS LIMIT
Less than 65 years of age	$7,080
65 to less than 70 years of age	9,720
At least 70 years of age	No limit

These limits increase each year. Each January the Social Security Administration will notify you of the new outside earnings limits. Also, if there are any other changes that affect the amount of the Social Security benefit, the Social Security Administration will notify potentially affected recipients immediately.

With regard to outside work in which a Social Security recipient engages, each January the Social Security Administration will send the recipient a form, called "Annual Report of Earnings," which must be filed by April 15. In September, Social Security will notify the recipient again

76

about revising the estimate of outside earnings for the current year, which was previously made on "Annual Report of Earnings."

Each January the Social Security Administration sends Social Security recipients a Form SSA-1099, called a "Social Security Benefit Statement." It shows their Social Security benefits for the previous year. This form is used in filing federal income tax returns, if they meet the requirements necessary to file a return.

33

YOUR REPORTING REQUIREMENTS

The Social Security Administration imposes a number of reporting responsibilities on recipients. Although certain information may be reported to the Social Security Administration by other federal government agencies, such inter-agency reporting does not relieve a recipient of Social Security-imposed reporting requirements. In some situations, if changes are not reported in a timely manner or if the recipient makes false statements in reporting, penalties may be imposed ranging from a reduction in Social Security benefits to a fine or imprisonment. Accordingly, recipients should pay close attention to the following reporting responsibilities.

On the "Annual Report of Earnings" workers report their estimated outside earnings for the current year in addition to their actual outside earnings for the previous year. If during the year they are able to determine that their actual earnings will be higher or lower than the estimate, they should apprise Social Security of the change so that benefits can be adjusted (see Key 32).

Any change in address for the worker or others who receive Social Security benefits on the worker's record should be provided to the Social Security Administration as soon as possible.

Recipients who have chosen to have their Social Security checks deposited directly in a bank or other financial institution, and then move or change banks, must inform the Social Security Administration of the changes. Both the new and the old account numbers must be reported to the Social Security Administration.

Sometimes a Social Security recipient may begin receiving pension benefits from work that is not covered by Social Security, such as the federal civil service system and some state or local pension systems. In those cases, the Social Security benefit may have to be refigured or offset (see Key 45). Similar adjustments may have to be made if the amount of the worker's pension from one of these entities changes. In either case, whether such non-Social Security pension benefits are just beginning or are changing, the Social Security Administration must be notified.

In some cases of marriage or divorce, the Social Security Administration must be notified. If you are receiving Social Security benefits on your own account, the retirement benefits continue regardless of a change in marital status; thus, you need not notify the Social Security Administration of a change in marital status. But if you receive Social Security benefits on another person's account, you must notify the Social Security Administration if there is a change in that person's marital status. The effect on the Social Security benefits depends on the relationship with the person on whose account Social Security benefits are being paid.

For the spouse who is receiving Social Security benefits on a spouse's account, the Social Security Administration should be notified if the marriage ends in a divorce or an annulment. Normally Social Security benefits stop in the month in which the divorce decree or annulment becomes final, but there is a major exception: if the spouse receiving the benefits is at least 62 years old and was married to the person on whose account the benefits are being paid for at least ten years, the benefits will continue. This factor does not eliminate the requirement for notifying the Social Security Administration.

The Social Security benefits of a widow, widower, or surviving divorced spouse will continue after remarriage, as long as the recipient is at least 60 years of age. For others who receive Social Security benefits on another's account or work record, benefits normally cease when the marriage ends.

In certain situations, the Social Security Administration must be notified even though there is no effect on the Social Security benefits. For example, if you change your name, perhaps because of marriage, divorce, or court order, even though benefits may continue, the Social Security Administration nevertheless requires you to notify them of the name change. Similarly, if a child who is adopted and has a name change has been receiving Social Security benefits, even though the adoption may not cause the benefits to cease, the adopting parents must notify the Social Security Administration of the child's new name, the date of the adoption decree, and new address.

If you receive Social Security benefits because you care for a child who is under age 16 or a child who was disabled before age 22, you must notify the Social Security Administration of the child leaving your care, and provide the child's name and new address. Whether or not the caregiver's Social Security benefits will cease depends on the type of separation. If it is temporary, and the person continues to exercise parental control over the child, Social Security benefits may not be affected. On the other hand, if the person no longer has responsibility for the child, benefits will cease, continuing only when the child care resumes. In any event, the caregiver's Social Security benefits will stop when the youngest unmarried child reaches age 16, even though the child's benefits may continue.

There are special reporting responsibilities for Social Security recipients who live, work, or travel outside the United States. If they travel outside the United States for at least 30 days, they must notify the Social Security Administration of the name of the country or countries that they plan to visit, and the date on which they expect to leave the United States. The Administration will send them special reporting instructions on how to arrange for the Social

Security checks while they are out of the United States. The Social Security Administration must be notified upon the recipient's return to the United States, too.

Supplemental Security Income benefits are not paid to a person who is outside of the United States for any whole calendar month or at least 30 consecutive days. Moreover, benefits will not begin again until the person is back in the United States for 30 days.

Even if your travel outside the United States is for fewer than 30 days, you may not receive your Social Security checks. As of this writing, you cannot get a Social Security check if you are visiting Albania, Cuba, Democratic Kampuchea, North Korea, the Union of Soviet Socialist Republics (Russia), and Vietnam. If you are a U. S. citizen, you are retroactively entitled to the money accumulated during the time you were out of the country; if you are not a U. S. citizen, you are not entitled to the back checks.

34

FAMILY MEMBER BENEFITS

Members of a worker's family may be entitled to receive Social Security benefits when the worker retires or becomes disabled and begins receiving benefits.

A spouse may receive Social Security benefits at the age of 62. Planning is important, though, because a higher Social Security benefit may be available if it is based on the spouse's own Social Security working record. If the spouse of a retired or disabled person is caring for a child who is under age 16 or disabled, a Social Security benefit may be paid at any age.

Social Security benefits may be paid to a worker's children if they are unmarried and under age 18, under age 19 and a full-time elementary or secondary school student, or age 18 or older and severely disabled. As for the latter, the disability must have been incurred before the child reached age 22.

A child's benefit stops with the month before the child reaches age 18. However, if the child remains unmarried *and* is either disabled or a full-time elementary or secondary school student, then the child's benefit will continue. About five months before the child's 18th birthday, the recipient of the child's benefits will get a form explaining how benefits can continue.

Certain special rules apply to disabled children when they reach age 18. Disabled children can continue to receive Social Security benefits after they turn 18 provided they have a physical or mental condition that prevents them from performing substantial gainful work, *and* the condition is expected to last at least one year. If disabled children recover from a disability and Social Security benefits are stopped, benefits may be started again if they become disabled again within seven years.

Special rules also apply to children who reach age 18 and are students. As noted earlier, children can receive Social Security benefits until they reach 19, provided they continue to be full-time elementary or secondary school students. Even if Social Security benefits stop because the children are no longer students, these benefits can be started up again if the children return to school on a full-time basis *before* they reach age 19.

In one instance, a child who is a full-time student may even receive benefits beyond the 19th birthday. If the child's 19th birthday occurs during a school term, the Social Security Administration will continue benefits up to two months to allow the child to complete the school term. Also, a student can continue to receive Social Security benefits during a vacation period of *four months or less* if returning to school full time at the end of the vacation period.

The Social Security Administration requires notification if certain events happen to a full-time student who is receiving Social Security benefits, as in the following instances:

1. The student drops out of school.
2. The student changes from full-time to part-time status.
3. The student is expelled or suspended.
4. The student changes schools.
5. The student is paid by an employer for attending school.

A form is sent to the student at the beginning and end of each school year. Social Security benefits could be stopped if the form is not promptly returned to the Social Security Administration.

Regarding age determination, the Social Security system considers an individual to reach a given age the day before one's birthday. If the birthday is August 1, the Social Security Administration considers that 18 years of age has been reached on July 31. Consequently, unless the child remains unmarried and is either disabled or a full-time elementary or secondary school student, the Social Security benefits will stop on July 30. Even if the benefits for a child stop, they may resume if the child becomes disabled before reaching age 22 or becomes a full-time student prior to becoming 19.

Normally, the family member entitled to Social Security benefits is eligible for a benefit amount equal to 50 percent of the rate for the retiring or disabled worker. The normal benefit is based on a spouse's being at least 65 years old *or* caring for a minor or disabled child. If these conditions aren't met, the 50 percent rate is reduced a small percentage for each month before age 65. The minimum rate that applies is 37.5 percent and it applies if the spouse is 62 years old. However, a spouse caring for a child who is under age 16 or disabled is entitled to receive full benefits (that is, 50 percent of the rate for the retiring or disabled worker, regardless of the worker's age).

35

FAMILY MEMBER OPTIONS

There are several options for receiving Social Security benefits if one is entitled to receive the benefits because of a spouse's retirement. For example, an individual may be eligible for both his or her own retirement benefits as well as benefits as a spouse. Here, the spouse of the retired or disabled worker receives the higher amount. Retiring couples should be aware of this opportunity to maximize Social Security benefits.

Each of a worker's children who is entitled to Social Security benefits may receive up to 50 percent of the worker's full benefit; however, there is a limit on the amount of Social Security benefits paid to a family. Although the limit varies, generally it is about 150 percent to 180 percent of the worker's benefit rate. If the sum of the benefits paid on a worker's Social Security record exceeds the family limit, benefits for only the nonworking members of the family are reduced proportionately.

The divorced spouse of a worker may be entitled to receive Social Security benefits on the worker's Social Security record even though the worker is not yet receiving Social Security benefits. However, the worker must be at least 62 years old, and the divorced spouse must:

1. have been married to the worker for *at least ten years,*
2. be at least 62 years old,
3. be unmarried, and
4. be ineligible for an equivalent or higher benefit on his or her own *or* on someone else's Social Security record.

A divorced spouse can get Social Security benefits even if the worker is not retired. However, the worker and ex-spouse must have been divorced for at least two years.

A worker, the children, and a divorced spouse may all receive benefits on the worker's Social Security record. The fact that a divorced spouse is receiving benefits does not affect the amount of benefits that are paid to the worker and other family members.

36

AFTER BENEFITS BEGIN

A number of events may affect someone's Social Security benefits. Some examples include:
1. a move.
2. a marriage or a divorce.
3. a name change.
4. an income or earnings change.
5. the birth or adoption of a child.
6. the incarceration of a beneficiary.
7. leaving the United States.
8. the death of a beneficiary.
If any of the above events occurs, a person should immediately inform the Social Security Administration or Health Care Financing Administration (if covered by Medicare) about the change.

Sometimes the Social Security Administration may make a decision that affects recipients' eligibility for Social Security benefits or Supplemental Security Income benefits. When this happens, they will receive letters from the Social Security Administration apprising them of its decision. For people who disagree with the decision, there are various avenues of appeal (see Key 17). The decision can be appealed within the Social Security Administration and there are several levels of appeal available within the system. People who are not satisfied with the results they obtain within the Social Security System appeals process may take their cases to the federal courts.

Generally if people receive other pensions from work where they paid Social Security taxes, it does not affect their Social Security benefits. However, if they receive pension payments from work that was not covered by Social

Security, their Social Security benefits may be lowered or offset by the amount they receive (refer to Key 45). Examples of pensions from work that is not covered by Social Security are the federal civil service or some state or local government employment.

People who receive Social Security benefits may work and earn income other than that which they receive from Social Security. In some situations, their Social Security benefits are limited because of the amount of their non-Social Security earnings. However, for persons 70 years old or older, Social Security benefits will not be cut because of outside income.

Persons under age 70 who have other income, however, may have their Social Security benefits reduced. The earnings requirements are different, depending upon whether the person is collecting Social Security retirement, dependents, survivors, or disability benefits, or Supplemental Security Income benefits. The Social Security Administration requests that people collecting disability or Supplemental Security Income benefits report all of their income to the Social Security Administration.

If people who receive Social Security benefits are not able to handle their personal financial affairs, the Social Security Administration will make the check payable in the representative payee's name on behalf of the worker beneficiary. Certain responsibilities are imposed and the representative payee is required to use the Social Security or Supplemental Security Income benefits for the personal care and well-being of the worker beneficiary. Additionally, the payee is required to keep the Social Security Administration in-formed of any events that might affect the worker beneficiary's eligibility for benefits. Finally, the payee is required to file a periodic financial report with the Social Security Administration. This report explains how the benefits were spent.

37

NON-SOCIAL SECURITY INCOME: EXAMPLES AND LIMITATIONS

The definition of outside, or non-Social Security, earnings or income is critical because such earnings may cause Social Security benefits to be reduced. The Social Security Administration only counts earnings that the worker earns from a job or net profit if self-employed. Examples of *counted* earnings include compensation such as bonuses, commissions, and vacation pay. Items *not counted* include pensions, annuities, investment income, interest, income from insurance, Social Security benefits, veterans' benefits, and government benefits.

Income is considered only when it is earned—not when it is paid. Deferred income that a retiree receives due to accumulated sick or vacation pay, bonuses, stock options, and other deferred compensation is not counted for purposes of the earnings limit in the year in which it is received.

If you have deferred compensation paid to you by a former employer, you should first ensure that it is reported by the employer in Box 14, "Nonqualified Plan," on your W-2 Form. The Social Security Administration subtracts this amount from your total earnings, which they count toward the earnings limit. If your employer does *not* report deferred compensation in Box 14 of your W-2 Form, contact the Social Security Administration before filing the required annual amount with them, and apprise them of the deferred compensation. By contacting them in advance, you may be able to avoid an unjustified cutback in your Social Security benefits.

For persons age 70 and older, there is no loss of Social Security benefits because of outside earnings. For persons under age 70 who receive Social Security retirement, dependents, or survivors benefits, the outside earnings limits vary, depending upon how old they are. If they were under age 65, the worker may have earned up to $7,080 in 1991 without having Social Security benefits affected. For each two dollars of outside income over $7,080, however, one dollar of Social Security benefits is lost.

Assume that Mary Adams is fully covered by Social Security and retires at age 62. She receives 80 percent of her full retirement benefits, or $1,022 per month, which amounts to $12,264 on a yearly basis. She continues to do some other work after retirement, earning $7,000 in non-Social Security earnings. Her non-Social Security earnings will not affect the monthly benefits she receives from Social Security.

Now assume that Ms. Adams earns $10,000 from her other work, thus earning $2,920 over the limit ($10,000 − $7,080). Her Social Security benefits will be cut by $1,460 ($2,920 ÷ 2), and her Social Security benefits will equal $10,804 ($12,264 − $1,460) on a yearly basis.

If Sam Evans was at least 65 years old but not yet 70 in 1991, he could have earned up to $9,720 in non-Social Security income without having his benefits cut. The reduction in benefits is more lenient than the cutback for workers under age 65 who have excess non-Social Security earnings. The benefits are cut one dollar for every three dollars in outside earnings over the $9,720 limit.

If you have excess outside earnings, you are required to report them to the Social Security Administration. The appropriate form is SSA-7770 F6, "Annual Report of Earnings," which can be obtained from your local Social Security office or by calling 800-2345-SSA. A penalty could be imposed if excess earnings are not reported by April 15 of the year following an excess-earnings year.

If the worker has outside earnings and family members receive benefits on that Social Security record, the total family benefits are affected by the worker's outside earnings. Both the worker's benefits *and* the family's benefits are reduced because of excessive non-Social Security earnings by the worker. However, if the worker does not have outside earnings but a family member works and has other earnings, only the family member's Social Security benefits are reduced.

38

PLANNING WITH NON-SOCIAL SECURITY INCOME

Two things need to be considered regarding the implications of outside earnings. The first is the cutback in Social Security benefits itself. Although you may be able to increase your outside earnings, your total income may not increase dollar for dollar because of the cutback in your Social Security benefits. Second, no more than one-half of your Social Security benefits will be subject to federal income taxes, but if your total earnings are below a certain amount, none of the Social Security benefits are taxed (see Key 40). It is more likely that all of your outside earnings will be subject to federal income taxes.

Assume that Tom Jones is 66 years old, is married, and files a joint federal income tax return. Mr. Jones has been receiving a monthly Social Security retirement benefit of $1,000, or $12,000 a year. He had three options for outside earnings in 1991: (1) he could have earned outside wages of $30,000; (2) he could have earned $25,000; or (3) he could have earned $9,720.

Under the first option, Mr. Jones received outside earnings in excess of $9,720, so his Social Security benefits were reduced. The excess was $20,280 ($30,000 – $9,720). His Social Security benefits were reduced by $6,760 ($20,280 ÷ 3). Therefore, his Social Security benefits became $5,240.

Mr. Jones had total income of $35,240 ($5,240 + $30,000). Since his income exceeded $32,000, $1,620 of the Social Security benefits were taxed. Mr. Jones paid federal income tax of $3,048. His net income, after federal income taxes, was $32,192 ($30,000 + $5,240 – $3,048).

Under the second option, Social Security benefits were also reduced because outside earnings exceeded $9,720. The reduction was not as much as under the first option. The excess was $15,280 ($25,000 − $9,720); and the reduction was $5,093 ($15,280 ÷ 3). Therefore, Social Security benefits became $6,907. Mr. Jones had total income of $31,907 ($6,907 + $25,000). None of his Social Security benefits were taxed. His federal income tax was $2,055 in 1991. His net income, after considering federal income taxes, was $29,852 ($25,000 + $6,907 − $2,055).

Under the third option, the Social Security benefits were not reduced because they did not exceed $9,720. Therefore, his Social Security benefits remained $12,000. None of his Social Security benefits were taxed. His federal income tax was $1,563. His net income, after considering federal income taxes, was $20,157 ($9,720 + $12,000 − $1,563).

The results of the three options are displayed below.

OPTION	INITIAL TOTAL INCOME	NET INCOME	DIFFERENCE
1	$42,000	$32,192	$9,808
2	37,000	29,852	7,148
3	21,720	20,157	1,563

The differences in net income are more pronounced as outside earnings increase to the point that they put a taxpayer in a higher tax bracket. In these three situations, Mr. Jones was always in the 15 percent tax bracket.

Each taxpayer must make a decision about the value of additional outside income. In these examples, we showed how net income is affected from lost Social Security benefits and partially taxed Social Security benefits (Option 1) to no lost Social Security benefits and no taxed Social Security benefits (Option 3). Compare the results in Options 1 and 3, and note that even though $20,280 more in outside income was earned under Option 1, only $12,035 more in net income resulted.

39

SPECIAL CONSIDERATIONS FOR NON-SOCIAL SECURITY INCOME

There is a special rule that applies in the first year that a worker is retired. Additionally, the annual outside earnings limitation is applied differently. The reason is that a worker who retires in the middle of the year may earn more than the yearly earnings limit in the months worked before retiring. A worker is entitled to receive full monthly Social Security benefits as long as outside earnings for the month are less than the monthly average of the annual outside earnings limitation. A full Social Security check may be paid for any whole month in which the worker is retired, regardless of the yearly earnings. For those months in which the worker is not fully retired, the regular yearly limit is applied on a monthly basis.

For example, recall (from Key 37) that if the worker is at least 65 years old but under 70, up to $9,720 in non-Social Security income may be earned in 1991 without having benefits cut. The $9,720 annual amount represents $810 monthly ($9,720 ÷ 12). In the worker's first year of retirement, if monthly earnings are $810 or less, full benefits will be paid. (The monthly earnings limitation for 1991 was $590 for workers under the age of 65.) This special rule applies, even though the worker may receive more than the annual limitation amount.

Here is a more specific example that illustrates this special rule. Assume that Alice Cobb turned 65 years old in August 1991 and became fully retired. Monthly earnings from employment were $4,000. After retirement, she had no outside income.

Cobb's outside earnings for 1991 would be $28,000 (7 months × $4,000 per month). This amount exceeds the permitted annual amount of $9,720 for workers between 65 and 70 years of age. Here, however, since Cobb had no outside earnings for the months of August through December of 1991, her benefits for those months was not affected. In fact, she could have had outside earnings of as much as $810 for each of the months of August through December, and still not have lost any Social Security benefits.

If the worker is self-employed, any services performed in that business are taken into consideration in computing monthly outside earnings. This special rule also applies to the $7,080 annual outside earnings limitation for workers who are under 65.

One of the guidelines used by the Social Security Administration to assess whether or not self-employed workers perform substantial services in their businesses is the amount of time they spend working. Generally, if self-employed persons work more than 45 hours a month, they are not considered to be "retired" for Social Security purposes, but if they work fewer than 15 hours a month in self-employment, they are considered to be retired. If they work between 15 and 45 hours a month in self-employment, they may or may not be retired based on the Social Security Administration's assessment of the work as substantial or not substantial. (Work is considered substantial if the self-employed workers are engaged in occupations requiring some skill, or if they manage a fairly large business.) This area is nebulous, and requires consultation with the Social Security Administration. Self-employed persons who want to support retirement status for Social Security purposes should keep good records with details of any work they do in self-employment.

If you earn more than the earnings limits for the ages specified in Key 37 and you receive Social Security benefits, the Social Security Administration requires submission of an "Annual Report of Earnings." Recall that if you are at least 70 years old, there is no outside earnings limit, and therefore the "Annual Report of Earnings" need not be completed.

On the "Annual Report of Earnings," you are required to show your exact earnings for the previous year and to give an estimate of your earnings for the current year. If you do not wish to complete the form, you may call your Social Security office and report your earnings over the telephone.

The "Annual Report of Earnings" must be returned by April 15 of the following year, the filing deadline for federal individual tax returns, but filing a federal individual tax return does *not* take the place of filing the required annual report of outside earnings with the Social Security Administration. There is a penalty for not filing the report on time. If you have an outside earnings limitation problem, call the Social Security Administration's toll-free number, 800-2345-SSA, and request the form if you have not received one by the end of February. If the Administration knows that you are working and that you receive some Social Security benefits during the year, you will automatically be sent the "Annual Report of Earnings" form.

40

DETERMINING IF SOCIAL SECURITY BENEFITS ARE TAXABLE

If a worker has no earnings other than Social Security benefits, no federal income taxes are due on the benefits. A worker in this situation will not likely have to file a federal income tax return.

Conversely, if a worker has earnings or income in addition to Social Security benefits, federal income taxes may be due on some part of the Social Security benefits. However, in no case will the worker have to pay federal income taxes on more than one-half of the Social Security benefits. The worker should use the "Social Security Benefit Statement" sent from the Social Security Administration to determine the amount of Social Security benefits received.

If you do not have to file a Form 1040 except for the fact that federal income taxes must be paid on part of the Social Security benefits, then you may choose to report the taxable Social Security benefits by filing the Short Form 1040A instead. Filing Form 1040A is simpler and easier than filing Form 1040.

Federal income tax is not withheld on Social Security benefits. Therefore, if a worker has outside earnings or income in addition to Social Security benefits, estimated taxes may be due during the taxable year. Obtain Publication 505, *Tax Withholding and Estimated Tax,* from the Internal Revenue Service, or the instructions for Form 1040-ES," Estimated Tax for Individuals."

If you receive Social Security benefits for yourself and a child, you must distinguish between the benefits received.

This distinction is important because Social Security benefits, if taxable, are included in the taxable income of the person who has the legal right to receive the benefits. If you receive a check that is for Social Security benefits for yourself and a child, only the part of the check that is for your own benefits is used in determining if any part of the Social Security benefits is taxable. The part of the check that is for the child's benefits is added to the child's other income in determining if any part of the child's Social Security benefit is taxable.

For the 1991 taxable year, Social Security benefits were not taxable if the recipient's income was not more than the following base amounts. At this writing, the amounts are the same for 1992. When you compute total income to compare against the following base amounts, only one-half of the Social Security benefits is included. The base amount is:
1. $25,000 if the person is single (including heads of households and qualifying widows and widowers).
2. $25,000 if the person is married, does not file a joint return, and did not live with a spouse at any time during 1991.
3. $32,000 if the person is married and filed a joint return in 1991.
4. $0 if the person is married, does not file a joint return, and did live with a spouse at any time during 1991.

If the worker is married and files a joint return with a spouse, the two must combine their non-Social Security incomes and one-half of their Social Security benefits to determine if any of their combined benefits is taxable. Even if the worker's spouse did not receive any Social Security benefits, the couple must include the spouse's income to determine if any part of the worker's Social Security benefits is taxable.

Assume that a worker and spouse file a 1991 joint federal income tax return. The worker's net Social Security benefits are $6,600, and the spouse's net benefits are $2,400.

The worker also received taxable pension income of $10,000 and taxable interest income of $500.

The couple's total income is $15,000, for purposes of determining if any portion of their Social Security benefits is taxable. The $15,000 equals one-half of their Social Security benefits, $4,500 (1/2 × [$6,600 + $2,400]), plus the $10,000 pension income plus $500 interest income. Since the $15,000 is less than the $32,000 base amount above, none of the $9,000 of Social Security benefits is taxable.

41

COMPUTING THE TAX IF BENEFITS ARE TAXABLE

If a worker's total income, including tax-exempt interest, exceeds the base amounts specified in Key 40, some of the Social Security benefits will be taxable. The amount that is taxed is the *lesser* of:

1. one-half of the Social Security benefits that are received during the year, and
2. one-half of the excess of the worker's "modified adjusted gross income" plus one-half of the Social Security benefits over the base amount.

Assume the same facts as in the illustration in Key 40, except that instead of a $10,000 taxable pension, the worker has $30,000 of taxable pension income. First, determine if any of the Social Security will be taxable. The couple's total income is $38,000 for purposes of determining if any of their Social Security benefits is taxable. The $35,000 equals one-half of their Social Security benefits, or $4,500 (1/2 × [$6,600 + $2,400]), plus the $30,000 pension income plus $500 interest income. Because the $35,000 is more than the $32,000 base figure, some of the $9,000 of Social Security benefits is taxable.

Next, compute the part of the Social Security benefits that is taxable. The taxable amount is the *lesser* of:

1. one-half of the Social Security benefits that are received during the year (this amount is $4,500), and
2. one-half of the excess of the worker's modified adjusted gross income plus one-half of his Social Security benefits over the base amount. The worker's modified adjusted gross income is $30,500 ($30,000 + $500). One-half of the Social Security benefits is $4,500. The sum of these

two amounts is $35,000, and the base amount is $32,000. The excess is $3,000 ($35,000 − $32,000), and one-half of the excess is $1,500.

Therefore, $1,500 of the Social Security benefits is included in taxable income and is subject to federal income tax.

Basically, this complicated tax system excludes most Social Security benefits received by lower- and middle-income people, but taxes up to one-half of the same benefits received by higher-income taxpayers.

The amount of the net Social Security benefit is in Box 5 of Form SSA-1099, which is sent to Social Security recipients. Form SSA-1099 is the "Social Security Benefit Statement."

The lump-sum death benefit paid by the Social Security Administration is not taxable, although other lump-sum benefits may be taxable. There are special rules for other lump-sum benefits. A person with a lump-sum benefit that is not a one-time death benefit should consult the Internal Revenue Service's Publication 915, *Social Security Benefits and Equivalent Railroad Retirement Benefits,* with respect to handling the federal income tax implications of such a payment. The Internal Revenue Service's Publication 554, *Tax Information for Older Americans,* may also be helpful for details on the taxability of Social Security benefits. Call the Internal Revenue Service's toll-free telephone number, 800-829-3676, to obtain these and other Internal Revenue Service publications.

42

CHECKING YOUR EMPLOYER'S MATH

Today, payroll administration is more complex than ever before. Even though computerized payroll software packages are being used by most firms, people still must enter the data, and occasionally human errors occur. Furthermore, even electronic systems sometimes develop glitches in programming. It is a good idea to occasionally verify the computations associated with your paycheck.

Most people work at least 40 hours a week and get paid every two weeks or once a month. When you look at your paycheck, you are concerned primarily with the bottom line—the net amount or take-home pay. Few people consider computing their paycheck to see if the employer has properly calculated the various deductions and net pay.

Social Security is one of the most significant deductions from workers' gross pay. Since Social Security tax is a major deduction, workers should know how it is computed and what benefits it provides. Social Security tax is withheld from the paycheck of virtually every working individual. This tax was established to fund a government program that provides for the economic security and social welfare of the American worker and family.

The Social Security tax is also known as FICA (Federal Insurance Contribution Act) tax. The FICA tax rate from 1990 to 1992 was 15.3 percent. This tax amount (rate) is divided equally between the employee and the employer. The employee has 7.65 percent of gross earnings withheld from the paycheck and the company/employer is responsible for paying the remaining 7.65 percent of the FICA tax. The tax is applied to every dollar earned up to a maximum amount (called the base amount). In 1991, the base amount was $53,400 for the retirement, disability, and survivors programs. For 1992, the base amount is $55,500. For Medicare, after 7.65 percent is paid on the first $53,400 of a worker's wages, 1.45 percent is paid on the remaining wages up to $125,000. The $125,000 figure was raised to $130,200 for 1992. Therefore, the maximum amount of Social Security tax (including Medicare) in 1991 was $5,123.30 and for 1992, $5,328.90.

Here is a planning point for self-employed persons. The self-employment tax rate is twice the rate for employees. The rate is 15.3 percent on the first $53,400 of net earnings from self-employment and 2.9 percent on earnings from $53,400 to $125,000 (see Key 4). If a self-employed person anticipated earning at least $250,000 over two years, that individual could save self-employment tax by keeping earnings under $125,000 in one year and exceeding $125,000 the next year. If a self-employed taxpayer had $125,000 of self-employment earnings in each of the 1991 and 1992 tax years, the total tax would be $20,493.20. If earnings can be controlled, for example $75,000 in 1991 and $175,000 in 1992, the total tax is $19,043.20. By deferring $50,000 of earnings, $1,450 in self-employment tax is avoided.

43

SPECIAL CIRCUMSTANCES FOR THE CLERGY

Ministers who have not taken a vow of poverty occupy a dual tax status under the tax laws. They are self-employed for Social Security purposes and employees for other tax and fringe benefit purposes. Clergy taking a vow of poverty are exempted from paying Social Security tax on earnings for services performed for the church. A minister may apply for an exemption from self-employment tax on all of the self-employment income (see Key 4 for self-employment tax calculations). The special circumstances of ministers under the Self-Employment Contributions Act (SECA) program may have resulted in huge losses of tax revenues from people generally thought to be above reproach.

The law allows ministers, rabbis, and priests to exclude the "fair rental value" (including utilities and certain other costs) of church-owned housing and/or portions of a household/furnishings allowance from gross income for income tax purposes. However, these income items are included in a cleric's net earnings for computing self-employment tax. There is a major difference, not generally well understood by laypeople or even many IRS agents, between the fair rental value income and the housing/furnishings allowance income. The latter is to be reported by the employer on a Form W-2 or a Form 1099, but the fair rental value is not.

The minister, if in the SECA program, is required to include the fair rental value in income reported on Schedule SE (Form 1040) for Social Security purposes, but there is no way for this figure to be cross-checked against any employer-reported amount. Therein lies the opportunity for uninformed clerics to innocently evade significant amounts of SECA taxes by failing to report or by grossly underreporting the fair rental value income. There is no separate line on Schedule SE for fair rental housing; the minister will need to indicate at the bottom of the page, as a footnote, what this contributes to reported SECA income.

Ministers are, in general, treated as employees for income tax and Form W-2 reporting purposes, but they are self-employed for Social Security purposes. In addition, in most cases they are exempt from the withholding tax provisions. Accordingly, the employers (churches or synagogues) have no way of checking the amount of income tax or Social Security tax actually paid by the ministers.

In addition, the law does not require the employer (church) to furnish the minister with the amount of the fair rental value income. It is entirely the responsibility of the minister to establish this amount each year by using "one percent per month of the professionally appraised value of the furnished home" or some "other reasonable means" of determining the value, considering the neighborhood and location, plus employer-paid utilities and other allowed costs. This value, even for modest housing, generally would be $10,000 or more per year, with corresponding SECA taxes of at least $1,530 (at 1991 rates).

When a home is not provided, a housing/furnishings allowance may be paid to the clergy by the church. Such an amount may be excluded from gross income to the extent used to provide a home or pay utilities for the home. The excludable housing allowance may not exceed the reasonable compensation for the services of the minister. The church must officially designate the payment as a housing allowance before the payment is made and not at a later date, and a definite amount must be so designated.

44

GOVERNMENT PENSION OFFSET

There are a number of instances in which a person may be eligible to receive Social Security benefits *and* other government-associated benefits. For example, a retired worker may receive retirement benefits from a federal, state, or local government that were not covered by Social Security. As another example, a spouse of a worker who is covered by Social Security may receive Social Security benefits on the worker's Social Security record and also receive an additional federal, state, or local government pension that is based on work not covered by Social Security. In both cases, the recipient of Social Security benefits may have those benefits cut back due to the other pension. A "government pension offset" reduces the Social Security benefits that a spouse receives on his or her own personal Social Security work record.

It is easier to understand the offset if you understand the Social Security Administration's reason for having it. Consider the situation in which a wife receives Social Security retirement benefits based on her own Social Security work record. Assume that her husband also did work covered by Social Security and he receives a Social Security retirement benefit. Recall that Social Security has a program under which the wife could be eligible to receive Social Security retirement benefits based on her husband's Social Security work record. However, her benefit normally is offset by the amount of any benefits she receives based on her *own* earnings that are covered by Social Security.

The government pension offset is designed to achieve the same result. The government pension offset affects a person who receives a federal, state, or local government pension based on work not covered by Social Security and who might be eligible for a spouse's, widow's, or widower's benefit from Social Security. The government pension offset rules also might affect widows and widowers who receive Social Security benefits based on another's Social Security work record.

Two-thirds of the recipient's pension is offset against the Social Security benefits that are received as a spouse. When the recipient takes the pension as a lump sum, Social Security computes the offset as if the recipient had chosen to receive the lump sum through regular monthly payments.

Assume that a husband has worked in jobs covered by Social Security all his life. Assume that his wife has worked for state government, which provides its own pension benefits, but is not covered by Social Security. Both the husband and wife are the same age and they retire at the same time.

The man receives a monthly Social Security benefit equal to $900. The two of them are scheduled to receive a total Social Security retirement check of $1,400, $500 of which would be due his wife in retirement. The wife also receives a $600 monthly benefit from her state pension. Two-thirds of her state pension, or $400 ($600 × 2/3), would be offset against her scheduled Social Security benefits on her husband's work record. Therefore, the part of the Social Security check that covers her, $500, would be reduced by the $400 amount. Her part of the Social Security retirement check would then be $100, and the total Social Security check would be $1,000 ($900 for him, and $100 for her). Their total combined retirement benefits would be $1,600 ($1,000 from Social Security + $600 from the state).

The entire Social Security benefit that is intended to cover a spouse could be eliminated because of the size of the federal, state, or local government pension (based on work not covered by Social Security) that the spouse receives. In this case, could the spouse still get Medicare at age 65 based on the spouse's work record? The answer is yes. Even though a spouse may not get cash benefits on a spouse's work record, the spouse can still get Medicare at age 65 based on that work record.

There are a number of exemptions to the government pension offset rules. The spouse whose work is not covered by Social Security but who could receive Social Security benefits based on the spouse's work record is exempt, and full Social Security benefits could still be received in the following situations:

1. The government pension is based on work that, on the last day of employment, *is* covered by Social Security.
2. The government pension is not based on earnings.
3. The person received or was eligible to receive the federal, state, or local government pension before December 1982, and the person met all of the requirements for Social Security spouse's benefits in effect in January 1977.
4. The person received or was eligible to receive the federal, state, or local government pension before July 1, 1983, and the person was receiving at least one-half support from the spouse.
5. The person is a federal employee who is mandatorily covered under Social Security.
6. The person is a federal employee who switched from the Civil Service Retirement System to covered employment before January 1, 1988 (if the switch was made after December 31, 1987, the person needs five years of federal employment that is covered by Social Security in order to be exempt from the government pension offset rules).

Remember that the government pension offset rules cover persons who might be able to receive Social Security benefits based on their spouse's Social Security work record. Key 45 covers the potential loss of those benefits when the worker who is covered receives a pension that is from work *not* covered by Social Security.

45

PENSIONS FROM WORK NOT COVERED BY SOCIAL SECURITY

There are situations in which a retired worker may receive more than one retirement (or disability) benefit. If one of the benefits is from Social Security and at least one other is a pension from work not covered by Social Security, a modified formula is used to figure the amount of the Social Security benefit. The key is that the worker receives a pension from a job not covered by Social Security and also has enough credits to qualify for Social Security retirement or disability benefits. The modified formula causes the Social Security benefits to be reduced, but the other pension benefits will not be affected.

The reason for the modified formula is the way Social Security benefits were computed before a 1983 change in the Social Security law. Previously, workers who worked only part of their lives in jobs covered by Social Security had their benefits computed as if they were long-term, low-wage workers, even though that may not have been the case. Historically, low-wage workers have always received larger Social Security benefits (compared to their earnings) in relation to higher-paid workers.

The modified formula is used to figure the worker's Social Security benefit beginning with the first month in which both a Social Security benefit and a pension from work that is not covered by Social Security is received. The modified formula affects workers who reach age 62 or become disabled after 1985, and first become eligible after 1985 for a monthly pension that is based in whole or in part on work not covered by Social Security. The Social Security rules specify that a worker is considered eligible to receive a pension if the requirements of the pension are met, *even though* the individual continues to work.

In a number of cases, the modified rule will not apply, and Social Security benefits will *not* be cut back. Here are the exceptions:

1. The worker is receiving survivors benefits.
2. The worker is a federal worker who was hired after December 31, 1983.
3. The worker was employed on January 1, 1984, by a nonprofit organization that was mandatorily covered under Social Security on that date.
4. The worker's only pension is based on railroad employment.
5. The worker's only employment where Social Security taxes were *not* paid was before 1957.
6. The worker has at least 30 years of "substantial" earnings under Social Security. "Substantial" earnings are those that are at least as much as amounts specified by the Social Security Administration from 1937 through 1991. The table below shows "substantial" amounts for selected years.

YEAR	SUBSTANTIAL EARNINGS AMOUNT
1950	$ 900
1955	1,050
1960	1,200
1965	1,200
1970	1,950
1975	3,525
1980	5,100
1985	7,425
1990	9,525

Under the regular formula used to calculate Social Security benefits, benefits are based on the worker's average monthly earnings adjusted for inflation. Those earnings are separated into three amounts, which are then multiplied by separate factors. (See Key 13.)

For example, when Social Security computes the retirement benefits for a woman who turned 65 years old in 1991, it multiplies the first $319 of her average monthly earnings by 90 percent, the second $1,603 by 32 percent, and the rest of her average monthly earnings by 15 percent.

Under this modified formula, the 90 percent factor is reduced to 40 percent for workers who reach 62 years of age or become disabled after 1989. However, the 90 percent factor is not reduced if the worker has at least 30 years of substantial earnings (item 6 above). For workers who have had more than 20 years of substantial earnings, the 90 percent factor will be reduced more than 40 percent, going from 85 percent for 29 years of substantial earnings to 45 percent for 21 years of substantial earnings.

The Social Security rules build a protective element into the modified formula, designed to protect workers who have relatively low pensions. The protection ensures that the cutback in the Social Security benefit under the modified formula will not be more than one-half of the part of the worker's pension that is attributable to earnings after 1956 that are not covered by Social Security.

QUESTIONS AND ANSWERS

Q. Where is my local Social Security office?
A. Check in your local telephone directory under "U.S. Government" or "Social Security Administration." You may also call the Social Security Administration's toll-free telephone number 800-2345-SSA, and ask for the address of the local Social Security office.

Q. A person may receive Social Security benefits and Supplemental Security Income benefits for a disability. Are the rules for determining disability different under those two programs?
A. No. The Social Security and SSI rules for determining disability are the same. You must be unable to do *any* kind of work to be considered disabled under both programs.

Q. Are other rules under the Social Security and Supplemental Security Income programs the same?
A. No, some rules are different. For example, there is a five-month waiting period before one can begin receiving Social Security disability benefits but a person can begin receiving SSI disability benefits right after applying. Also, the rules are different for people with disabilities who want to go back to work.

Q. When will I receive my Social Security check?
A. Social Security benefits are paid on the third day of the month. If the third falls on a weekend, a Monday, or a holiday, benefits will be paid on the previous Friday. Sometimes there is a delay by the post office in delivering checks. The Social Security Administration suggests that

you wait for three working days after the normal delivery date before you report a lost check to them.

Q. I want to have my Social Security check deposited directly into my bank account. How do I arrange for that?

A. Call the Social Security Administration to have your Social Security check directly deposited into your bank account. The telephone number is 800-2345-SSA. Have information about your financial institution readily available, including name and address, your account number, and other names on a joint account. The Social Security telephone representative will request information about your Social Security claim number and information about your bank.

Q. How do I change my address?

A. Call the Social Security Administration at 800-2345-SSA. They will want at least the following information: your new address, ZIP code, new telephone number, and Social Security claim number.

Q. How will I know what benefits to report on my income tax return?

A. At the end of the calendar year, the Social Security Administration will send you Form SSA-1099, the Social Security Benefit Statement. The statement shows the amount of benefits you received in the previous year. Some part of your benefits may be taxable *only* if you have income from other sources.

Q. What can I use to show proof of what I received from Social Security?

A. The above-mentioned Form SSA-1099, the Social Security Benefit Statement, can be used as proof of what you received from Social Security.

Q. How do I get a new Social Security card or Medicare card?
A. Call the Social Security Administration at 800-2345-SSA for your new card. You could also visit your local Social Security office. In either case, have your Social Security number available.

Q. Why is my friend's Social Security check more than mine?
A. The computation of Social Security benefits depends on a number of variables. For example, a person's date of birth and complete work history will affect the amount of the Social Security benefits. It is unlikely that two people have the same birth dates and work histories and therefore unlikely that two people will receive the same Social Security check. The Social Security Administration protects the privacy of each person and will not give out information about the records of others.

Q. I recently received a letter from the Social Security Administration. I do not understand it. How can I get an explanation of the letter?
A. The Social Security Administration's telephone representatives should be able to answer questions about any letters or other correspondence you receive from them. First, check the letter for any local (or other) number to call. If there is none, call Social Security's toll-free number 800-2345-SSA.

Q. How much can I earn this year in non-Social Security earnings before my benefits will begin to be reduced?
A. For 1991, the earnings limits were $7,080 for people under age 65, and $9,720 for people 65 to 69 years old. At 70 years of age, there are no outside earnings limits. Call the Social Security Administration if you need to revise your earnings estimate.

Q. Are my benefits figured on my last five years of earnings?

A. While some private pension plans base retirement benefits on earnings from selected years (for example the worker's last five years, the worker's three highest years, etc.), Social Security retirement benefits are based on the worker's *total* earnings during a lifetime of work under the Social Security system. Years of high earnings will increase the amount of the retirement benefit, but no group of years counts more than any other.

Q. Will the retirement pension from my job reduce the amount of my Social Security benefit?

A. If your private pension is from work where you also paid Social Security taxes, the amount of your private retirement pension will not affect the amount of your Social Security benefit. However, pensions from work not covered by Social Security (for example, the federal civil service or some state or local government systems) probably *will* reduce the amount of your Social Security benefit.

Q. What does Medicare cover?

A. *The Medicare Handbook* contains detailed information about the services covered by Medicare. Your *Handbook* should arrive in the mail near the time when your Medicare entitlement starts. If you do not receive a *Handbook,* call the Social Security Administration's toll-free number 800-2345-SSA.

Q. What are the parts of Medicare?

A. Medicare has two parts: hospital insurance and medical insurance. *Hospital insurance* helps to pay for inpatient hospital care and certain followup care and is referred to as Part A. *Medical insurance* helps to pay for your doctor's services and many other medical services and items and is referred to as Part B.

Q. What does the hospital insurance part of Medicare cover?

A. There are four major areas of hospital insurance coverage: inpatient hospital care, inpatient care in a skilled nursing facility, home health care, and hospice care.

Q. What does the medical insurance part of Medicare cover?

A. There are four major areas of medical insurance coverage: doctors' services, outpatient hospital services, home health visits, and other medical and health services.

Q. What are some items that Medicare does not cover?

A. Some of those items are custodial care (for example, help with bathing, eating, and taking medicine), dentures and routine dental care, certain appliances (such as eyeglasses, hearing aids, as well as examinations to prescribe or fit them), nursing home care (except for care in a skilled nursing facility), personal comfort items (for example, a telephone or television in one's hospital room), prescription drugs, most routine physical checkups and related tests, and hospital or medical services received outside of the United States.

Q. Do I have the medical insurance part of Medicare, or the hospital part of Medicare?

A. To determine the parts of Medicare that you have, look at the entries on your red, white, and blue Medicare card. If you see the words, "Medical Insurance," or "Medical (Part B)," you are covered for the medical part of Medicare.

Q. How do I file a Medicare claim?

A. You do not need to worry about filing a Medicare claim. The service providers (doctors, hospitals, medical laboratories, etc.) handle the submission of Medicare claims.

Q. What are the documents I will need to apply for my Social Security benefits?

A. When applying for any Social Security benefit, you may need to provide your Social Security card, your birth certificate, your children's birth certificates if they are applying, your marriage certificate if you are signing up for Social Security benefits on your spouse's Social Security record, and your most recent W-2 form (or your tax return if you are self-employed). If you do not have the original documents, you will need to have your copies certified by the issuing office.

Q. When should children obtain Social Security cards?

A. The 1990 tax law requires that all dependents who are at least one year old at the end of the year must have a Social Security number, and that number must be shown on the parent's federal income tax return. You should obtain a Social Security card for your child soon after birth.

Q. How do I obtain a Social Security card for my children?

A. Contact your local Social Security office and complete Form SS-5, "Application for a Social Security Card."

Q. What documentation will I need to obtain a Social Security card for my children?

A. If you are getting a card for the first time, you should have a birth certificate and some other form of identification. With respect to the birth certificate, you should have the original document (or a certified copy) because the Social Security Administration will not accept uncertified copies. Check with the hospital where your child was born because some hospitals automatically make application for the newborn. Other forms of identification for a newborn child may include a doctor or hospital bill.

117

Q. How may I obtain an estimate of my Social Security benefits when I retire?

A. To request a specific estimate of your Social Security benefit, obtain Form SSA-7004, "Request for Earnings and Benefit Estimate Statement," call 800-2345-SSA or check in your local telephone directory under "Social Security Administration" or "U.S. Government."

Q. Should I verify my Social Security record with the Social Security Administration?

A. It is a good idea to verify your Social Security record every three years. The reason is to make sure you are getting credit for all of your earnings. If you are not, the sooner you verify any inaccuracies, the easier it will be to correct them.

Q. What is the SSI program?

A. SSI is the abbreviation for Supplemental Security Income, a program designed for certain workers. If you have not accumulated enough Social Security credits to qualify for Social Security, you may be eligible for the SSI program and, if your benefit from Social Security is very small, you may also be eligible for the SSI program. If you believe that you might qualify for SSI benefits, contact the Social Security Administration at 800-2345-SSA.

Q. What is normal retirement age for Social Security retirement benefits?

A. If the worker retires at full retirement age, now 65, he or she will be eligible for full retirement benefits. If the worker retires earlier, benefits may be reduced. Finally, the worker's Social Security benefits may also be affected by late retirement.

Q. Specifically, how will my Social Security retirement benefits be affected if I delay my retirement?

A. You may decide to retire later than the full retirement age, which is now 65. Two considerations must be taken into account regarding *late retirement*. First, depending on what you earn each year beyond the normal age for Social Security retirement, your average earnings may be increased and that increase could result in an increase in your Social Security benefit when you retire. Second, there is a special credit for workers who delay retirement that creates an increase in their retirement benefits. The increase is based on a certain percentage and is automatically added from the time the worker reaches full retirement age until benefits are begun or 70 years of age is reached, whichever comes first. The special credit varies, depending on birth date. For workers who turned 65 in 1991, the percentage was 3.5 percent for each year beyond normal retirement age. The percentage will increase in the future until it reaches 8 percent per year for workers who turn 65 in 2008 or later.

Q. How much are Social Security retirement benefits if I retire early?
A. If the worker retires before full retirement age 65, benefits may be reduced. If the worker retires at age 62, the reduction in the monthly check is 20 percent; at age 63 the reduction is 13-1/3 percent; at 64 it is 6-2/3 percent.

Q. What are some examples of situations in which disability benefits may be received under Social Security?
A. Disability benefits may be received for:
1. a worker who has earned sufficient Social Security credits to qualify on his or her own work record.
2. the disabled widow or widower of a spouse who had earned sufficient Social Security credits to qualify on his or her own work record.
3. a worker with low income and few assets who might be eligible for Supplemental Security Income benefits.
4. a child over age 18 who might be eligible based on the parent's work record.

5. a child of any age who might be individually eligible for Supplemental Security Income benefits.

Q. How does the Social Security Administration determine if you qualify for benefits under its disability program?
A. The Social Security Administration has its own process to determine if you are disabled, which involves the answers to five questions: (1) Are you working? (2) Is your condition severe? (3) Is your condition found in the list of disabling impairments? (4) Can you do the work that you previously did? (5) Can you do any other type of work?

Q. Who may receive Social Security benefits on a deceased worker's Social Security work record?
A. Various family members may be able to collect Social Security payments on a deceased worker's record. Here are some examples: (1) one's widow or widower who is at least 60 years old; (2) one's widow or widower who is at least 50 years old *and* disabled; (3) one's widow or widower, regardless of age, caring for a child who is either under age 16 or is disabled; (4) unmarried children under age 18; (5) unmarried children age 18 or 19 who are full-time elementary or secondary school students; (6) unmarried children over age 18 who are severely disabled and the disability began before the child was 22 years old; (7) parents, if they were dependent on the deceased worker for most of their support; and (8) one's divorced widow or widower, if the widow or widower is not eligible for an equivalent or higher benefit on his or her own record.

Q. How can I find out how much Social Security I have paid into the system?
A. Every three or four years you should obtain Form 7004 from the Social Security Administration by calling your

local Social Security office or the Social Security Administration's toll-free number 800-2345-SSA. Fill out the form, send it in, and in about 30 days the government will tell you the amount of your earnings since 1950. They will also tell you your estimated retirement benefits and your estimated disability benefits. This action on your part can catch any errors in your Social Security account and help you plan for your retirement.

Q. What benefits may I expect to receive after paying my FICA taxes for many years?
A. Benefits that a worker may expect to receive after paying the employee's portion of the FICA tax during his or her working years fall into four categories:
1. old age or disability benefits paid to the individual worker.
2. benefits paid to the dependents of a retired or disabled worker.
3. benefits paid to surviving family members of a deceased worker.
4. lump-sum death payments.

With each of these benefits, an individual may immediately begin receiving them as soon as eligibility requirements have been met. Benefits are based on an employee's average monthly wages. In a few situations, benefits may be denied (for instance, a retired employee may earn more than a prescribed amount or an individual may be convicted of certain crimes). To apply for benefits, go to your local Social Security office.

GLOSSARY

Annual Report of Earnings the form mailed out each January by the Social Security Administration to those who receive Social Security benefits. Recipients must specify on the form the amount of their outside earnings. The form is to be filed by April 15.

Appeals Council the third level of appeal for one who disagrees with a Social Security Administration decision on a disability claim. If the Appeals Council determines that there is an issue the judge did not address at the lower appeal level, it will review the case. At this point, all levels of appeal within the Social Security Administration are exhausted. If the Appeals Council denies the review because it believes that all issues have been addressed by the judge at the hearing level of appeal, or the Appeals Council renders a decision with which you disagree, you must appeal to a federal civil court to continue the appeals process. If you have not previously engaged an attorney, one should be retained now.

Asset test used under the SSI program to determine if the potential recipient of SSI benefits has low enough assets to qualify.

Base amount fixed amounts used to determine if a taxpayer who receives Social Security payments must pay tax on part of the payments. The amounts are $32,000 if a married taxpayer files a joint return, zero if a married taxpayer files a separate return, and $25,000 for all others.

Benefit period under the Medicare program, the period that begins the day you enter a hospital and ends when you have been out of a hospital or skilled nursing facility for 60 consecutive days.

Blindness for purposes of qualifying to receive benefits under Social Security's disability program, blindness means that vision cannot be corrected to better than 20/200 in the better eye, or the visual field is 20 degrees or less, even with corrective lenses.

Coinsurance under the Medicare program, the percentage beyond the deductible amount for which Medicare picks up the approved charges for covered services in a particular year. For example, with an 80 percent coinsurance provision beyond the deductible amount, Medicare would cover 80 percent of the medical services in question.

COLA See "Cost-of-living raises."

Cost-of-living raises a provision in the Social Security law under which the benefit is increased automatically if the cost of living rises. Also referred to as COLA for "Cost-of-Living Adjustments."

Covered services the specific services under Medicare for which a part or total insurance payment will be made.

Credits Social Security credits determine one's eligibility for Social Security programs. A person earns credits by working in a job covered by Social Security and by paying Social Security taxes. In 1991 one credit was earned for each $540 in Social Security earnings. A maximum of four credits can be earned in a year.

Deductible the initial amount of a medical expense that the worker is required to pay before Medicare begins to make payments. For example, for 1990 Medicare hospital insurance, there was a $592 deductible, so the worker was responsible for the first $592 of hospital costs.

Direct deposit a convenient means by which Social Security recipients may receive their checks. The checks are deposited directly into the bank or financial institution of their choice.

Disability physical or mental impairment that must keep a person from doing any "substantial" work for at least one year, *or* a condition expected to result in the person's death.

The person must qualify to receive payments under Social Security's disability program. Under this definition, Social Security does not cover a disability that is temporary or short-term.

Disability program one of five programs in the Social Security System under which monthly payments are made to a disabled worker who has enough Social Security credits. Other family members of a qualifying worker may also receive disability payments under the disability program.

Disability work incentive incentives under the Social Security disability program that encourage disabled workers to return to work. The four specific incentives are trial work period, extended period of eligibility, deductions for impairment-related expenses, and Medicare continuation.

Earnings Social Security earnings are the most important factor used to determine the amount of your Social Security benefits. Benefits are based on earnings (adjusted annually for inflation) averaged over most of the working lifetime. Verify the amount of your earnings at least every three years by completing Form 7004-PC and mailing it to the Social Security Administration.

Enrollment period under Medicare's Part B medical insurance protection, there is an initial enrollment period of seven months during which you may sign up for the coverage. This *initial enrollment period* begins three months before the month in which you first become eligible for the medical insurance protection and ends three months after that month. For people who do not sign up for the medical insurance protection during their initial enrollment period, there is a *general enrollment period,* during which they can subsequently enroll, January 1 through March 31 of each year. For the person who applies during a general enrollment period, protection begins the following July.

Extended period of eligibility one of four specific incentives under the Social Security's disability program to encourage disabled workers to return to work. Under this incentive, if the worker is still disabled for 36 months after a successful trial work period, he or she will be eligible to receive a monthly benefit without a new application for any month that earnings drop below $500.

Federal Insurance Contribution Act the Federal law that provides for the imposition of the Social Security tax. Also referred to as FICA.

FICA See "Federal Insurance Contribution Act."

Form 7004-PC See "Request for Earnings and Benefit Estimate Statement."

Form HA-501 a form used to request a hearing because of a disagreement with a Social Security Administration decision affecting a claim.

Form SS-5 also referred to as "Application for a Social Security Card." It is used to obtain a Social Security number, a lost Social Security card, or change the name on a Social Security card.

Form SSA-1 F6 a form used to apply for retirement insurance benefits under Social Security.

Form SSA-2 F6 a form used to apply for a spouse's insurance benefits under Social Security.

Form SSA-4 BK a form used to apply for a child's insurance benefits under Social Security.

Form SSA-5 F6 a form used to apply for a mother's or father's insurance benefits under Social Security.

Form SSA-8 F4 a form used to apply for a lump-sum death payment under Social Security.

Form SSA-10 BK a form used to apply for a widow's or widower's insurance benefits under Social Security.

Form SSA-1099 See "Social Security Benefit Statement."

Form SSA–7770 See "Annual Report of Earnings."

Free-look provision the period of time that insurance companies are required to give a customer to review a Medigap policy. During this period, the customer may return the policy to the agent or company if it is not wanted.

Freeze a provision of the Social Security disability program under which a blind person who is able to work and have "substantial" earnings (and not qualify for Social Security disability benefits) will not have future benefits reduced because of relatively lower earnings in the years when the person was blind. Under a freeze, the lower earnings years (when one was blind for Social Security purposes) will not be incorporated into the Social Security benefit calculation model.

Full retirement age for Social Security purposes, the retirement age at which full retirement benefits will be received. Full retirement age is now 65. At retirement earlier than 65, the Social Security retirement benefit will be reduced. If retirement occurs later than full retirement age, the benefit may be increased in some instances.

General enrollment period See "Enrollment period."

Government pension offset a provision in the Social Security law under which a person's benefit received on a spouse's work record is reduced because that person is eligible for a federal, state, or local government pension based on his or her own work record and that pension is based on work not covered by Social Security.

HCFA See "Health Care Financing Administration."

Health Care Financing Administration a division of the U.S. Department of Health and Human Services. It administers the Medicare program.

Hearing the second level of appeal by one who disagrees with a Social Security Administration decision on a disability claim. Under the *hearing* level of appeal, a worker is entitled to apply for a hearing before a judge.

Impairment-related expenses work expenses related to one's disability. One of the Social Security disability program's incentives for encouraging disabled workers to return to work is to discount impairment-related expenses when it is determined that a disabled worker's earnings constitute substantial work.

Income test used under the SSI program to determine

whether the potential recipient of SSI benefits has a low enough income to qualify.

Initial enrollment period See "Enrollment period."

Levels of appeal the various steps available to one who disagrees with a Social Security Administration decision on a disability claim. It applies to other types of claims as well. The four usual levels of appeal are reconsideration, hearing, appeals council, and U.S. district court.

Medicaid a health insurance program designed for people who have low income and limited assets. It is usually run by state welfare or human service agencies. A person may qualify for both Medicare and Medicaid or for only one of the programs.

Medicare one of five programs under the Social Security System in which hospital and medical insurance coverage is provided to those who are covered. It is run by the Health Care Financing Administration, although the Social Security Administration takes applications for Medicare, assists beneficiaries in claiming Medicare payments, and provides information about the program. Medicare is a basic health insurance program that covers people who are 65 years old or older, people of any age with permanent kidney failure, and certain disabled people, regardless of their age.

Medicare continuation one of four specific incentives under the Social Security's disability program to encourage disabled workers to return to work. Under this incentive, the disabled worker's Medicare coverage will continue for 39 months beyond the trial work period. If the worker's Medicare coverage stops after returning to work, the worker may purchase it for a monthly premium.

Medicare hospital insurance also referred to as Medicare Part A. A monthly premium is not required in order to receive this coverage if the worker or spouse is entitled to benefits under either the Social Security or Railroad Retirement Systems, or worked a sufficient period of time in federal, state, or local government employment to be insured.

Medicare hospital insurance helps pay for medically necessary services furnished by Medicare-certified hospitals, skilled nursing facilities, home health agencies, and hospices.

Medicare medical insurance also referred to as Medicare Part B. Part B is optional but a monthly premium is required in order to receive this coverage. It is offered to all beneficiaries when they enroll in Part A. Medicare medical insurance helps to pay for physician services and many other medical services and supplies that are not covered by Medicare Part A.

Medigap types of health insurance policies designed to cover the areas of noncoverage under Medicare. Examples of noncoverage areas targeted by Medigap policies are the deductibles under the Medicare insurance policy, coinsurance amounts specified in the Medicare insurance policy, medical charges that exceed Medicare's approved amounts, and various medical services and supplies not paid for by Medicare.

Modified adjusted gross income the amount of a taxpayer's adjusted gross income from federal Form 1040, without certain income/deductions that are normally included/deducted. Modified adjusted gross income is used to determine if a Social Security recipient who has other income is required to pay tax on Social Security income. Social Security payments are normally not taxable.

Outside earnings non-Social Security income that a Social Security recipient earns. Social Security places restrictions on the amount of outside earnings that one who receives Social Security benefits may have. Beyond these restrictions, benefits are cut back and sometime even eliminated.

Reconsideration the first level of appeal by one who disagrees with a Social Security Administration decision on a disability claim. Reconsideration entitles the worker to have a decision reviewed by persons other than those who made the original decision.

Representative payee a person who receives Social Security payments on behalf of a worker/beneficiary who is not able to handle financial affairs.

Request for Earnings and Benefit Estimate Statement a Social Security Administration form that can be used to obtain an estimate of Social Security benefits. This form may be used to verify Social Security earnings. Also referred to as Form 7004-PC, it may be obtained from your local Social Security office or by calling 800-2345-SSA.

Reserve days the 60 extra hospital days that one can use if a long illness necessitates a stay in the hospital of more than 90 days. These days are part of the Medicare hospital insurance program (Part A) and are called reserve days. They are not renewable like the 90 hospital days in each benefit period. Once used, they are gone.

Reserves there are two financial sides of the Social Security System—the contributions taken in and the expenditures to implement the System's programs. When contributions exceed expenditures, an excess results, known as "reserves." The excess is invested in Treasury bonds.

Retirement program one of five programs in the Social Security System under which monthly payments are made to retired workers who have enough Social Security credits. Payments may also be made to the retired worker's spouse.

SECA See "Self-Employment Contributions Act."

Self-Employment Contributions Act the Federal law that provides for the imposition of the Self-Employment tax. Also referred to as SECA.

Self-employment income the income of self-employed persons. A self-employed person's income is covered by Social Security if net profit from the trade or business is at least $400 for the year. The self-employed person pays taxes on earnings in excess of the $400. In some instances, a person's self-employment income may count for Social Security even if actual net earnings are not at least $400.

Social Security Benefit Statement Form SSA-1099, mailed

out each January to Social Security recipients. The form shows the benefits for the previous year and is used in filing federal income tax returns (if requirements are met that make filing necessary).

Social Security Act the federal retirement plan enacted by Congress in 1935. The original purpose (unchanged today) of the Act was to adopt a system that required the current working generation to contribute to the support of older, retired workers. The Act was passed in response to old-age dependency resulting from Depression-generated phenomena.

SSI See "Supplemental Security Income."

Substantial gainful activity See "Substantial work."

Substantial work the extent of work in which one is engaged when Social Security will stop payments under the disability program. (The Social Security Administration also refers to substantial work as "substantial gainful activity.") "Substantial" indicates that the work involves productive physical or mental activities and "gainful" means that the work is done for pay or profit. Normally, earnings of $500 or more a month constitute a substantial gainful activity. A determination by the Social Security Administration that the worker is engaged in a substantial gainful activity will not, however, affect any benefits that the recipient might be receiving under the Supplemental Security Income program.

Supplemental Security Income also called SSI, one of five programs in the Social Security System under which monthly payments are made to people with both low income and few assets. Disability payments may also be made under the SSI program. Although run by the Social Security Administration, SSI is not financed by Social Security taxes or trust funds but by general revenue funds of the U.S. Department of the Treasury.

Survivors program one of five programs in the Social Security System under which a lump-sum payment and monthly payments are made to a qualifying worker's survivors.

Teleservice center a convenient operation of the Social Security Administration for answering questions. There are thirty-seven teleservice centers throughout the country, which can be reached by dialing (800) 2345-SSA. In addition to answering general questions, the centers can provide the phone number of your nearest local Social Security office.

Trial work period one of four specific incentives in the Social Security's disability program to encourage disabled workers to return to work. Under this incentive, a disabled worker may earn as much as possible for nine months without having any Social Security disability benefits affected. The nine months do not have to be consecutive. However, the nine months of work must be within a five-year period in order to be considered a trial work period.

United States District Court the fourth and last level of appeal for a worker who disagrees with the Social Security Administration's decision about a worker's disability or other Social Security ruling. The U.S. District Court is a court of original jurisdiction within the federal court system. A worker can appeal an unfavorable decision by the district court to the Circuit Court of Appeals. The only recourse after the circuit court is to appeal to the U.S. Supreme Court. Unlike the district court and circuit court, which must hear the worker's case if it is filed, the Supreme Court may or may not decide to hear the worker's case.

Waiting period the length of time that must elapse before payments begin under a Social Security program. For example, under Social Security's disability program, disability payments do not begin until the sixth full month in which the person is disabled.

INDEX

Making the Most of Your Maturity With...

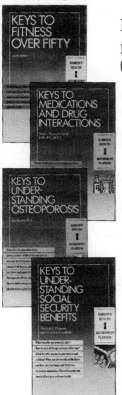

Barron's Keys to Retirement Planning

Each Key: Paperback: $5.95, Canada $7.95
(and $6.95*)

Keys To...

Buying a Retirement Home Friedman & Harris
(4476-2)*

Choosing a Doctor Lobanov & Shepard-Lobanov
(4621-8)

Dealing With the Loss of a Loved One Kouri (4676-5)

Fitness Over Fifty Murphy (4514-9)*

Living With a Retired Husband Goodman (4705-2)

Medications and Drug Interactions Gever
(4749-4) *NEW*

Nutrition Over Fifty Murphy (4512-2)

Planning for Long-term Custodial Care Ness (4593-9)

Preparing a Will Jurinski (4594-7)*

Understanding Arthritis Vierck (4731-1)

Understanding Medicare Gaffney (4638-2)

Understanding Osteoporosis Rozek (4664-1) *NEW*

Understanding Social Security Benefits
Dickens & Crumbley (4466-5) *NEW*

Plus a comprehensive single volume of friendly general advice...

Life Begins at 50: A Handbook for Creative Retirement Planning
by Leonard Hansen
Tips on retirement living, including handling your money prudently, knowing about available health care, Social Security and Medicare benefits, finding fun and bargains in travel and entertainment. Paperback: $11.95, Canada $15.95, 352 pp., (4329-4)

Barron's Educational Series, Inc.
250 Wireless Blvd., Hauppauge, N.Y. 11788
Canada: Georgetown Book Warehouse
34 Armstrong Ave., Georgetown, Ont. L7G 4R9

Prices subject to change without notice. Books may be purchased at your bookstore, or by mail from Barron's. Enclose check or money order for total amount plus sales tax where applicable and 10% for postage and handling (minimum charge of $1.75, Canada $2.00). ISBN PREFIX: 0-8120